"A NEW SPIRIT,
A NEW COMMITMENT,
A NEW AMERICA"

"A NEW SPIRIT, A NEW COMMITMENT, A NEW AMERICA"

THE INAUGURATION OF

PRESIDENT JIMMY CARTER

AND

VICE PRESIDENT WALTER F. MONDALE

THE 1977
INAUGURAL COMMITTEE

DUOBOOKS

"A New Spirit, A New Commitment, A New America"
The 1977 Inaugural Committee / DuoBooks, Inc.
Copyright © 1977 by the 1977 Inaugural Committee
Printed in the United States of America
All rights reserved
Library of Congress Catalog Card Number 77-70043
ISBN 0-918394-01-5

"I, Jimmy Carter, do solemnly swear
that I will faithfully execute
the Office of President of the United States,
and will to the best of my ability,
preserve, protect and defend
the Constitution of the United States.
So help me God."

THE OATH OF OFFICE

The Inaugural Address

"THE AMERICAN DREAM ENDURES"

For myself and for our nation, I want to thank my predecessor for all he has done to heal our land.

In this outward and physical ceremony we attest once again to the inner and spiritual strength of our nation. As my high school teacher, Miss Julia Coleman, used to say, "We must adjust to changing times and still hold to unchanging principles." Here before me is a Bible used in the inauguration of our first President in 1789, and I have just taken the oath of office on the Bible my mother gave me just a few years ago, opened to a timeless admonition from the ancient prophet Micah: "He hath showed thee, O man, what is good; and what doth the Lord require of thee, but to do justly, and to love mercy, and to walk humbly with thy God?"

This inauguration ceremony marks a new beginning, a new dedication within our government and a new spirit among us all. A President may sense and proclaim that new spirit, but only a people can provide it. Two centuries ago our nation's birth was a milestone in the long quest for freedom. But the bold and brilliant dream which excited the founders of this nation still awaits its consummation. I have no new dream to set forth today, but rather urge a fresh faith in the old dream. Ours was the first society openly to define itself in terms of both spirituality and human liberty. It is that unique self-definition which has given us an exceptional appeal. But it also imposes on us a special obligation to take on those moral duties which, when assumed, seem invariably to be in our own best interest. You have given me a great responsibility: to stay close to you, to be worthy of you, and to exemplify what you are. Let us bring together a new national spirit of unity and trust. Your strength can compensate for my weakness, and your wisdom can help to minimize my mistakes. Let us learn together and laugh together and work together and pray together, confident that in the end we will triumph together, in the right.

The American dream endures. We must once again have full faith in our country and in one another. I believe America can be better. We can be even stronger than before. Let our recent mistakes bring a resurgent commitment to the basic principles of our nation, for we know that if we despise our own government, we have no future. We recall in special times when we have stood briefly but magnificently united. In those times no prize was beyond our grasp. But we cannot dwell upon remembered glory. We cannot afford to drift. We reject the prospect of failure or mediocrity or an inferior quality of life for any person. Our government must at the same time be both competent and compassionate. We have already found a high degree of personal liberty, and we are now struggling to enhance equality of opportunity. Our commitment to human rights must be absolute, our laws fair, our natural beauty preserved. The powerful must not persecute the weak, and human dignity must be enhanced. We have learned that *more* is not necessarily *better*, that even our great nation has its recognized limits, and that we can neither answer all questions nor solve all problems. We cannot afford to do everything, nor can we afford to lack boldness as we meet the future. So together, in a spirit of individual sacrifice for the common good, we must simply do our best.

Our nation can be strong abroad only if it is strong at home. And we know that the best way to enhance freedom in other lands is to demonstrate here that our democratic system is worthy of emulation. To be true to ourselves we must be true to others. We will not behave in foreign places so as to violate our rules and standards here at home. For we know that the trust which our nation earns is essential to our strength. The world itself is now dominated by a new spirit. Peoples more numerous and more politically aware are craving and now demanding their place in the sun, not just for the benefit of their own physical condition, but for basic human rights. The passion for freedom is on the rise. Tapping this new spirit, there can be no nobler, no more ambitious task for America to undertake on this day of a new beginning than to help shape a just and peaceful world that is truly humane.

We are a strong nation, and we will maintain strength so sufficient that it need not be proven in combat—a quiet strength, based not merely on the size of an arsenal but on a nobility of ideas. We will be ever vigilant and never vulnerable. And we will fight our wars against poverty, ignorance and injustice, for those are the enemies against which our forces can be honorably marshaled. We are a proudly idealistic nation. But let no one confuse our idealism with weakness. Because we are free, we can never be indifferent to the fate of freedom elsewhere. Our moral sense dictates a clear-cut preference for those societies which share with us an abiding respect for individual human rights. We do not seek to intimidate, but it is clear that a world which others can dominate with impunity would be inhospitable to decency and a threat to the well-being of all people.

The world is still engaged in a massive armaments race designed to insure continuing equivalent strength among potential adversaries. We pledge perseverance and wisdom in our efforts to limit the world's armaments to those necessary for each nation's own domestic safety. And we will move this year a step toward our ultimate goal: the elimination of all nuclear weapons from this earth. We urge all other people to join us, for success can mean life instead of death.

Within us, the people of the United States, there is evidence of serious and purposeful rekindling of confidence. And I join in the hope that when my time as your President has ended, people might say this about our nation: that we had remembered the words of Micah and renewed our search for humility, mercy and justice; that we had torn down the barriers that separated those of different race and region and religion, and where there had been mistrust, built unity with a respect for diversity; that we had found productive work for those able to perform it; that we had strengthened the American family, which is the basis of our society; that we had insured respect for the law, and equal treatment under the law for the weak and the powerful, for the rich and the poor; and that we had enabled the people to be proud of their own government once again. I would hope that the nations of the world might say that we had built a lasting peace based not on weapons of war but on international policies which reflect our own most precious values.

These are not just my goals, and they will not be my accomplishments but the affirmation of our nation's continuing moral strength and our belief in an undiminished, ever-expanding American dream.

Thank you very much.

A PRESIDENCY WITH THE PEOPLE

Reflections upon a unique institution

by JAMES DAVID BARBER

In the great sweep of history, the American Presidency is new. Ages went by with most of humanity clear out of the picture of rulership, asleep to the affairs of state, seldom even wondering what the king was doing tonight. The United States of America was meant to be different: a people ruling ourselves by means of a government made by us. The President is our First Servant. We expect him to know what the wiser and better parts of our nature would want the government to do, and to see to getting that done. We load him with duties and then stand back and watch. Those who were for him cheer, those who were against him squint.

Harry Truman said that "most Presidents have received more advice than they can possibly use," and he was right. People who would never presume to tell an engineer how to build a bridge or a surgeon how to transplant kidneys feel free to straighten out their President. Professors and journalists have probably been the worst offenders. Professors have the leisure to smoke out the lessons of the last war and apply them to the next one—a mode of reasoning that can lead to cavalry charges against concrete bunkers. Journalists these days, let in to watch the President change his socks and comb his hair, can't help but feel the urge to supply answers to questions the President ought to ask but hasn't thought of yet. And if you stick a microphone in the face of your average American citizen, who may have trouble remembering the difference between the Declaration of Independence and the Bill of Rights, you can usually get him or her to pass on some words of counsel and advice to the Chief Executive. Many a President has found the job a lonely one—yet at the same time complained, as Warren G. Harding did, that "I can't get away from the

9

men who dog my footsteps."

Now in these chancy times, citizens might well contemplate what a perilous course we have set for our servant and consider whether we, *with* him, might find a way to lend a hand.

The Republican Tradition: Plainness and Power

Two traditions have shaped the modern President's ways of being, a republican and a democratic tradition. The political parties with those names both aim to stand for both traditions.

The republican tradition came first. It grew out of a revolution against a meddling king and his high and mighty governors. The revolutionaries established a negative principle: no rule by a distant power in which we had no voice. The Constitution makers had the more complex task: to design a government, a "new order of the ages," strong enough to last, yet free of the terrors of tyranny. After considerable debate, they decided not to call the President "Majesty" or "Excellency" but "Mister President." He would serve not for life but for a set term, be elected not by his fellow governing leaders but by the citizenry, acting through a special electoral college. If he lurched beyond the bounds of the Constitution, he could be thrown out of office at any time. And the President was made dependent on the people's representatives for laws and money and, as it turned out, on independent judges who had the ultimate power to decide what the laws meant.

The men who drafted the Constitution wished to avoid the trappings of power surrounding European monarchs, typified by the English king against whom they had rebelled. Here is His Majesty George III, draped in fur, portrayed by Allan Ramsay.

At its birth, the Constitution was a theory. Its fathers hoped, despite deep doubts, that it would last a quarter-century or so, resting that hope mainly on the idea that if part of the system went wrong, the other parts would correct it. The task of making the theory work fell to a miscellaneous band of Congressmen, judges, soldiers, clerks, and to a President who, in the early years, floated from city to city looking for a permanent home. In 1790, a wrangling Congress finally delegated the choice of a capital city to President Washington; he placed it at the southernmost extreme of the territory allowed him. Early Washington, D.C., mocked Major Pierre L'Enfant's grand plan. It was a swampy, malarial little village in the woods, where Congressmen lived in boarding houses, leaving their families safely back home, a post where foreign diplomats hustled for some more civilized assignment, a place soon peopled by "a class of swaggering sycophants . . . for[cing] themselves into the presence of distinguished and well-bred people," as one of the latter put it. And all that *talk!* "Babeltown," they called it.

So the government got underway in a frontier town rather than in the elegance of New York or Philadelphia, and the Presidency got underway with a frontiersman. George Washington, for all his natural dignity, had been a hill-hopping surveyor, a farmer, a country squire. As President he saw "the glare which hovers round the external trappings of elevated office," but wrote that "to me there is nothing in it, beyond the lustre which may be reflected from its connection with the power of promoting human felicity." Washington the town and Washington the man left lessons by example for succeeding Presidents, especially the lesson an ancient king required to be repeated to him daily: "Remember, your Majesty, that you are mortal."

That theme of republican virtue, of plainness in the Presidency, lasted past the start. We see it in just-inaugurated Thomas Jefferson waiting his turn for lunch, in Abraham Lincoln's letter to a child who wanted him to grow a beard, in Eleanor Roosevelt serving hot dogs to the King and Queen of England, in Harry Truman washing out his own socks and underwear in the White House, in Gerald Ford toasting his morning muffin. From time to time Presidents forgot their mortality and got their egos tangled in the trappings, confused themselves with the Saviour or the sovereign. Eventually, though, the Presidency gets called back to its old republican homeplace.

Not that the Presidency was or is for weaklings. The republican tradition recognized the need for positive leadership. The Presidency became an engine of enterprise, not a home for retiring glad-handers. President Washington could be tough. He demonstrated to John Hancock, the big-signatured Governor of Massachusetts, that the President of the United States took precedence over any Governor, and he made the Senate understand that he, not they, would decide when he needed their advice and consent on foreign policy. Presidents henceforward, with too many sorry exceptions, have felt responsible for making the government move out to solve problems—which is, in a fast-moving world, the only way to preserve, protect, and defend the Constitution.

The Democratic Tradition: Bring in the People

What was incomplete in the republican tradition was power for the people. Only a minority of male, white, propertied people was allowed to vote in the first place, and the impact of their votes was muted and filtered through various representational indirections. Voters cast ballots for state legislators who, in turn, elected the U.S. Senators. In the first three Presidential elections, most of the electoral college was chosen by the state legislatures. The Bill of Rights—the price the founding fathers had to pay to get their Constitution accepted—inhibited abuse of power but came short of sharing power with the great body of the people.

That remained for the second of our great traditions, the democratic tradition, the impulse insisting that government "by the consent of the governed" meant more than passive approval of the best available inside deal. Jefferson was away in Paris when the Constitution was written; possibly he would have made the founders see the contradiction between the wide language of the Declaration and their narrow definitions of the franchise. It took generations and many hard, long, courageous struggles to get the laws fixed so that an eighteen-year-old black working girl could walk relaxed into the court house and cast her vote.

Laws work when people want them to. The democratic tradition

George Washington, unanimously elected first President, wore a plain black suit for his official portrait by Gilbert Stuart. For all his simplicity of dress, Washington put great stress on the dignity of the nation's highest office.

Overleaf: Early Washington was a marshy backwater, a chancy place to locate a seat of power. By the time this idealized lithograph was made in 1851, the city—and the office of the Presidency—had emerged from infancy. The Capitol dome as well as the House and Senate wings were actually still incomplete.

reached beyond the formal rules to the spirit, the nation's life blood and vital energy. Raucous General Andrew Jackson may not have had as wide a base of voters as was once thought, but he charged into the Presidency "like a cyclone from off the Western prairies," as Woodrow Wilson put it, and laid about him as the people's President. "His strength lay with the masses, and he knew it," his friend Martin Van Buren remembered. Let the people in—the White House furniture could be repaired. The country would never be the same. Equally important, what the country thought about the Presidency would never be the same.

Keeping the democratic tradition lively was imperative because it runs against a natural social tendency: for those in the know to get together and work things out to their own advantage. It is *so* much easier that way, so much quicker, so convenient and familiar and calming to the nerves. The President, like the rest of us, craves the surcease of anxiety. If he wants to, he can find calm in a little coterie of White House pals, spiced up from time to time by some old friend from the provinces. That is not just a Washington disease—at this moment, all over the country, cozy companionships of the powerful are cementing themselves, "successful" people are discovering that they speak the same language, and casually, the deals are going down. The democratic tradition moves against this trend, urges involvement and participation and access by more people in more government decisions—not only at the finish, but from the start. This is the inclusive impulse, the open government impulse, the sense that government is the community's business and that

More than any other President, Andrew Jackson (shown in a daguerrotype below taken just before his death) saw himself as a direct representative of the people. He opened the White House to mobs of supporters after his inauguration, an event caricatured in the lithograph at left by Robert Cruikshank.

the community is everybody—not just a companionship of the powerful.

From the beginning Presidents have hoped and claimed to speak for The People, for the nation as a whole against the special interest groups or privileged classes. The voice of the people is accepted as a secular version of the voice of God, and the President may see himself as a political John the Baptist. The President can and often does invoke The People against the conglomerate of their own representatives, against the newspapers, against the weight of informed opinion. Woodrow Wilson felt this urge most keenly: "Whatever strength I have and whatever authority I possess are mine only so long and so far as I express the spirit and purpose of the American people." But until very recently, no one had a very good way to find out what the people—the actual people as distinguished from The People as an idealized abstraction—had on their minds. Picking apart the election returns gave only the foggiest clues; for instance, we know now that a lot of voters cast their ballots *against* the Presidential candidate they dislike, leaving the winner with only a negative mandate—not to do what the other candidate would have done. Mass media and polling give the people a direct means of learning what the President is saying and doing and give a much clearer account of what we think we want. There is still a good deal of fog in the polls, but on dramatic public issues the President is constrained or empowered by what Gallup and Harris discover on the surface of the popular psyche.

The Bond of Sentiment: Leaning on the President

The democratic tradition is loud with exhortation: people should take part in politics, vote, speak up, get involved. Leaders harangue the nation's youth with this message. The old Greek word for "idiot," they remind us, referred to people who kept to private life and failed to exercise their civic duties. All that preaching comes from a fearsome fact: there are a lot of "idiots" among us, politically lazy folk who have their own fish to fry and are prepared to let the government cook itself. We tend to look to each new President as suddenly responsible for the nation's general welfare, all by his lonesome, as Henry V's soldiers looked to him:

> Upon the king! Let us our lives, our souls,
> Our debts, our careful wives,
> Our children, and our sins, lay on the king . . .

For the democratic Presidency is, in the public eye, much more than an "executive" office. For better or worse, we tie ourselves emotionally to our Presidents, even to the ones who falter and fail. We hunger for the President to reassure us that things are going to turn out all right, to serve as an inspiring example of the nation's ideals, to march at the head of the column in the attack on our troubles. In England, the Queen is there to absorb and express those deep feelings, leaving the Prime Minister relatively free to operate as a practical politician. Here all that falls on the President—and if he fails in *that* relationship, all his other castles fall.

This mysterious bond of feeling between the people and the President shows itself whenever a President dies in office. Most Americans still remember where they were when John F. Kennedy was cut down, and the way it felt—like a blow to the solar plexus—when we lost that fresh young contender. Researchers have found that the same wave of deep sadness swept through the people at every Presidential death in office: not only for Lincoln and Roosevelt, but for James Garfield, William McKinley, and poor Harding. By contrast, when *ex*-Presidents die there is but a respectful formal mourning.

Not that we are constant worshipers at a White House shrine. A better way of putting it is that Americans feel ambivalent, divided inside, about their Presidents. We rally round the President in a crisis and in the high hope of inauguration day, but, with a curious regularity, we also seem to like to raise a President up and then watch him fall. His popularity declines as he moves on the hard choices. His great purposes become less newsworthy than the fits and starts of his political experiments. Maybe something in us wants our most powerful champion to turn out to have feet of clay; maybe we are simply reacting to the truth that no lone two-legged human can possibly succeed as George Washington in today's Washington, D.C. In any case, the President is the lead actor in the national political drama. His other skills, however strong, won't save him if he is a bust in that role.

The people expect the President to keep the Constitutional faith, not only to leave law and liberty intact when he moves out of the White House, but also to use the formalities with a democratic spirit.

The Great Conversation: The Art of Honesty

Above all, the President is called upon to maintain the Great Conversation by which we discern, eventually, "ideas whose time has come." The dictators disdain chatterbox democracy, but our tradition depends on talk, on "reasoning together." When the great conversation breaks down, people fall into private dreams and public grunts, and the end of the democratic tradition is not far. If history is any guide, Presidents do their worst damage when they fall into a credibility gap—when their words no longer signify their intentions. The black lie in Presidential politics (as distinguished from the little white lies all of us tell every day) is a lie about where his mind is and where he is trying to take us. Theodore Roosevelt understood that well: "My value as an asset to the American People consists chiefly in the belief that I mean what I say." For all his troubles, Harry Truman left little doubt about what he was trying to say, and Dwight Eisenhower, despite his rambling rhetoric, came across as sincere—people felt they knew what he meant. Amazing but true: we speak the same language but we keep misunderstanding one another. Jefferson realized that truth-telling was not always easy. He said, "The whole of government is the art of being honest"—honesty required *art*. Given hundreds of millions of us potential misunderstanders, it also

Presidents sometimes are cruelly cartooned. At other times, they are sentimentally idealized. To deify Lincoln, the unknown creator of the work above simply substituted the 16th President's face for that of the first in the earlier painting on glass, "Apotheosis of Washington," opposite.

takes patience in explaining and an ear tuned in to hear the reaction.

Presidents have found need of Jefferson's art because so much of what they say is subject to selection and interpretation by other explainers. The American mass media are the envy of the world. In most nations, the press falls far short of our standard; of course, that does not mean that what we have is good enough for *us*. Presidents have seldom wound up with a favorable opinion of the press, having seen too many of their sacred cows butchered by reporters. Realistic Presidents know that while they can dominate the media (a determined President can almost always get his message out) and even by-pass the reporters (as FDR did with his fireside chats), still they are very dependent on the talkers and writers who tell the story day after day. Even in the "pop-up" Presidential press conference, where the President decides whom to recognize and when to change the subject, he is vulnerable to surprise and discombobulation as he stands up there winging quick answers to questions he cannot always anticipate. He can count on this or that little frightening phrase being ripped out of context and bannered on the evening's news. And he can be sure that the columnists, whose job it is to make reality simpler and more interesting than it really is, will, at times, find him flabbergastingly wrong. No President since Coolidge (who loved reporters) has ended up with the warm feeling that his portrait in the press was a masterpiece.

The printing press had its first great outpouring in an age of faith, in Martin Luther's time. You can still find people who justify their political sentiments by reference to something set down in black and white, as if the printing of it made it true. Television news became popular in the 1950's; we saw the Army-McCarthy hearings and the Kefauver crime investigation with our own eyes. The public uses both media casually, though not uncritically these days, but we swim in a sea of assertions beyond our power to test in any direct way. Therefore, the President we know, the only one we can know, is the President delivered to us in the morning paper and the evening news—a mediated President.

Presidents learn to use the press, to put the best face they can on the matter. Historically that has included a fair portion of fakery; the first "media event" no doubt happened long before Charlemagne crowned himself. But what tears up the President's nerves—even when he is not faking—is the double bind the press puts him in. Hard experience clarified that bind in Herbert Hoover's mentation: he saw his duty "to help the people of the United States to get along peacefully and prosperously without any undue commotion or trouble over their affairs," but the reporters kept pressuring him to "provide the press with exciting news of something about to happen." Reporters live by a cardinal rule: "Nothing is new for very long." Their pencils have to push, their cameras roll, lest we the people miss our daily dose of excitement and enlightenment.

Past Presidents have all grappled with the professional President-watchers, and sometimes won. Some reporters have let themselves be had, turned into flacks. But that goes against the H. L. Mencken tradition that the only way for a reporter to look at a politician is down. And if today's television entertainment is romantic fantasy (and what fun those wars were!), today's television news conveys a sense of suspicion, of selfish purpose behind the politician's apparent generosity, the lie behind his candid look, the blunder masked by his smooth exterior. The President has to live with a press set up to discover that he is seldom what he seems.

The trick is to give them their news, an unending parade of events, and to counteract skepticism with achievements that cannot be neglected. Modern Presidents can take comfort in the fact that they are not the first to be roasted in the press. Washington was cartooned as a strutting fop, Lincoln as a baboon, TR as a buck-toothed maniac, Franklin Roosevelt as a helpless cripple, and so it goes. The natural human reaction is to crawl back into your shell, repeating to yourself the old definition of the critic: the guy who comes down on the battlefield when the fight is over and shoots the wounded. That reaction can turn a President into a secretive sovereign, barricaded with his sycophants in the Oval Office, sucking the thumb of "public relations" as the bane and benison of his existence. Presidents who have been relatively successful with the press—and none has been wholly so—have done what they could to help reporters do their work, in the furtherance of the President's own purposes, and then let the devil take the hindmost, as President Roosevelt did, laughing over Westbrook Pegler's relentless diatribes as he read them aloud to his circle of reporters in the Rose Garden.

Presidential Progress: Catching the Political Imagination

Woodrow Wilson, a President who wrote better than he ruled, summed up the power Presidents can achieve if they succeed in connecting with and guiding forward the mainstream of national belief:

The President can dominate his party by being spokesman for the real sentiment and purpose of the country, by giving direction to opinion, by giving the country at once the information and the statements of policy which will enable it to form its judgments alike of parties and of men.

His is the only national voice in affairs. Let him once win the admiration and confidence of the country, and no other single force can withstand him, no combination of forces will easily overpower him. His position takes the imagination of the country. He is the representative of no constituency, but of the whole people.

Finding and holding positions that will capture the imagination of the country is hard to do, because the popular imagination, and the real experiences it grows out of, are in perpetual motion. The republican and democratic traditions are enduring themes, but there is in our memory and anticipation another theme that bucks against the whole idea of tradition—the theme of progress. Our history as a democratic republic is old; our political culture values newness of life, progress if possible, change in any case. We are a people always starting over again, from the New Zion planted in Plymouth to the waves of new Americans transported here, by their will or against it, to the eventual millions fanning

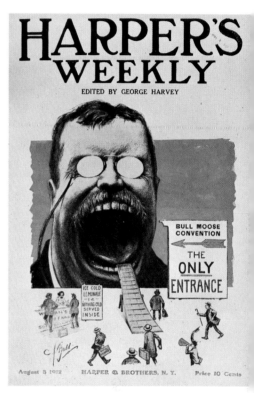

Presidents are never far removed from politics. In public print, they are often drawn and sometimes quartered. Opposite is "Long Abraham Lincoln," as he was depicted in 1864 *Harper's Weekly* cartoon. Many years later, Teddy Roosevelt was lampooned on the cover of that same magazine.

Calvin Coolidge was one of the few Presidents who loved the press. Although he reportedly disliked being photographed, Coolidge always obliged, as he did here in Rapid City, South Dakota, going western with a cowboy shirt, bandana, ten-gallon hat and chaps emblazoned with his name.

out across the landscape in search of a new chance, even a new identity. The cowhands used to sing "What Was Your Name in the East?" but from then to now each generation has its eyes fixed more on the future than the past.

To the President, that makes innovation a necessity. He will sink if he stands still. Born and bred in rapidly retreating days gone by, he struggles to catch up with present-day life and to lead us on into happier tomorrows. Thumbing through the history books in search of guidance, he finds tales running in every conceivable direction—how Lincoln, for instance, was tough and gentle, tragic and comic, sensitive and vulgar. If he consults the futurologists, he may find a Merlin, but is more likely to find a numerological trend-projector or a modern Delphic oracle high on gas. Part of him tries to capture the meaning of the time we are just emerging from; part of him has to lean against the "lessons" so confidently pronounced by experts in the hypothetical correction of deeds already done. They will help him see how fast the world turns; he must figure out in which directions he will try to nudge it.

John Jay, in *Federalist LXIV,* saw the opportunity hiding inside the apparent chaos:

They who have turned their attention to the affairs of men must have perceived that there are tides in them; tides very irregular in their duration, strength, and direction, and seldom found to run twice exactly in the same manner or measure. To discern and to profit by these tides in national affairs is the business of those who preside over them; and they who have had much experience on this head inform us that there

frequently are occasions when days, nay, even hours are precious.

All times try men's souls, but a President's own time will go down in history with his name on it. The popular tides seem sluggish or fickle as he ditches and dams. There was a time when the idea of votes for women was a bizarre speculation. Before this century runs out, we may well have a woman President. Successful Presidents have been midwives for such ideas whose time has come, though even the best of Presidents can radically misread the temper of his times, as Franklin D. Roosevelt did when he tried to pack the Supreme Court. That temper seems to move by action and reaction: a stolid William Howard Taft follows a vigorous TR and, in turn, gives way to a moralizing Wilson, and when Wilsonian uplift gets tiresome, it is time for an easygoing Harding. It is no accident, we can say with hindsight, that the big question Gerald Ford had to face was, Is he honest? Some Presidents grasp the current mood and manage to press forward. Others, like John Quincy Adams, find being President a "harassing, wearying, teasing condition of existence," a blur of "perpetual motion and crazing cares." Or, as the President tries to listen for what's going on, he may grump with Taft: "I'll be damned if I am not getting tired of this. It seems to be the profession of a President simply to hear other people talk." Or he can switch and twitch so rapidly, with every little jiggle of opinion, that he becomes, in Hoover's disdainful phrase about FDR, "a chameleon on plaid."

Roosevelt was no chameleon, he was an experimenter. Unsure about a lot of things, he knew, "One thing is sure. We have to do something. We have to do the best we know how at the moment. . . . If it doesn't turn out right, we can modify it as we go along." Feeling for a path out of the dark of the Depression, he stepped along vigorously and tentatively, ready to change course as need be.

Government as Navigation: Presidential Variations

"Government" comes from the Greek word for steering. To steer straight in modern politics requires feedback—monitoring the *results* of the steering, the actual effects of policies on the lives of the citizens. Hard as it is to get his program passed and beaten down into administration, the President may find it harder yet to determine what if any difference it all makes to the people. Polls help, but isolated, randomly selected pollees are themselves in a poor position to see the overall picture. It is up to The People's Choice to know what they would choose if they were he; we need the general's view, not the view from the foxhole. The war in Washington is too often a closet drama in which victory is proclaimed before the real battle is joined, out there in "the field." Congress has its hearings, for people who can take time off and get to Washington, and there are traveling Presidential commissions from time to time. But a severe and persistent problem, even today with all our sophisticated means of communication, is the President's intelligence: smart as he is, he will do dumb things if he is blind to the facts or relies on too many other second-guessers. Again, Roosevelt had it right when he told Rexford Tugwell, "Go and see what's happening. See the end product of what we are doing. Talk to people; get the wind in your nose." And the President must be prepared for bad news—not only the news of clean failure but the mushier news of maybe yes and maybe no. Being human, he would love to hear from the constituent who wrote FDR:

Dear Mr. President:

This is just to tell you that everything is all right now. The man you sent found our house all right, and we went down to the bank with him and the mortgage can go on for a while longer. You remember I wrote you about losing the furniture too. Well, your man got it back for us. I never heard of a President like you. . . .

But more important than the praise and damnation is knowledge—reliable, closely researched findings on what the input has done to the output. The big thinkers have yet to solve this one, though there is much good new research in progress. Meanwhile the President acts on what he has.

The President. This is the point at which to say that there is no "President," only Presidents, one after another, each equipped with such ways and means as history—his and ours—hands him. What kind of person a President is is important because the "office" (another abstraction) is so loosely defined. For all the advice a President gets, there is no manual for the job. He promises to be faithful in executing the office and to keep the Constitution. That document spells out some of his powers—what he *may* do but not what he *should* do when he runs up against situations X, Y, Z. On a discouraging note, the first mention of the President tells of the Vice President taking over, followed at once by the procedure for impeachment.

The Constitution's spare provisions were written in the confidence that George Washington would be the first of the series, and that he could be counted on to set the proper precedents. He tried, but many of the precedents he dwelled upon have long since passed into the archaic. For example, "Whether it would tend to prompt impertinent applications and involve disagreeable consequences to have it known that the President will, every Morning at eight Oclock, be at leisure to give Audience to persons who may have business with him?" Washington had to invent "the Presidency" from scratch. In important and trivial ways, so has each new President down to now.

Artemus Ward admired Washington's dignity: "Washington never slopt over." But slopping over has not been the only temptation—some Presidents have tried to dignify themselves right up through the clouds.

A popular myth, born of the union of a political religiosity and the vicarious hopes of the middle-aged, has it that the White House transforms its Chief Occupant, alchemizes him from politician to statesman. Chester A. Arthur is the usual example, a shady spoilsman (Wilson called him "a nonentity with sidewhiskers"), who, as President, turned on the bosses and got the Civil Service Act passed and implemented. On the other hand, dark-minded writers dwell on Lord Acton's cautious

Franklin Roosevelt felt the President needed to talk to the people he governed, to get their feedback, to "see what's happening." Here he meets North Dakota homesteader Steve Brown in 1936.

conundrum that "power tends to corrupt, and absolute power corrupts absolutely," an opinion for which there are more examples. A better way of putting it is that the Presidency tends to exaggerate a man. If he was gnawed by self-doubt before, the Presidency will make it gnaw harder—much harder. If he was a spoiled child grown large, his Presidential nature will feed on the psychological spoils so plentifully available. Give the Presidency to an essentially pontifical character—there to do his high, disagreeable duty—and he will find it possible to rise above all those tedious political fights. Or, with some luck and calculation, we may get a President who exaggerates the office's positive possibilities: a happy warrior, confident and vigorous, searching for ways to grow toward excellence and in the habit of forgiving himself when he fails.

Such subjects are, in fact, more appropriate to election day than to inauguration day. At election time—1980, 1984—we need to take a long, close look at the candidates, not just in the artificial flurry of campaigning, but in their lives and ways before the Presidential bug fastened on them. What Presidentially relevant skills have they demonstrated? What beliefs—about people, about history, and about political morality—have they brought to bear on their experience over the years? What basic character shapes their politics? We need to get past the little campaign bloopers a candidate makes and the whoppers he tells (which feed the lazy analyst in search of a magic sign) and ask who he is—and why. The best clues to that are in what he was in the warp and woof of his life experience. And one more thing: can he laugh at himself? The public President had to be a "solemn ass," according to Coolidge, though in private he himself was the wittiest since Jefferson, and most Presidents can get a humorous kick out of the foibles of their adversaries. But humor about the self, in moderation, can give him a little distance, a little valuable detachment, and is a symptom, I think, of inner strength, as when Lincoln compared his laughter to "the neigh of a wild horse on his native prairie."

Chester Arthur, elevated to office by the assassination of Garfield, is one of those who grew into the Presidency. Despite a reputation as a spoilsman, he drove out the bosses and reformed the civil service.

Mr. President Comes to Washington: Connecting with Congress

But of course the President is only one factor in the Presidential equation. He operates in a town full of egos with their own powers and purposes. A number of them think they could do his job better than he can. A significant few have it in mind to replace him at the first opportunity. And yet most have a strong stake in his success, not only because their political lives depend on that, but also because they care about the country and recognize how essential Presidential leadership is to national progress.

Citizens who despair over political fighting in Washington should recall that the separated powers are *supposed* to fight. The Constitution makers set it up that way, and generations of Washingtonians have fulfilled their expectation. They scattered responsibility and split up authority, so that no one power could lord it over the others for long. The sign on Harry Truman's desk—"The Buck Stops Here"—was wrong: the buck is all over town, and it moves from hand to hand. Illogical, yes. Inefficient, without a doubt. Surely *someone* has to have the last word? Not in our system: the words roll on, vibrating through a strangely sovereignless concatenation of semi-independent networks. Like kids tied together in a three-legged race, our government marches on legs from different bodies.

The system thus insures that the President will experience frustration. Congress, the major power at the other end of the street, will see to that if no one else does. Theodore Roosevelt once spoke softly of Congress: "I have a very strong feeling that it is a President's duty to get on with Congress if he possibly can, and that it is a reflection upon him if he and Congress come to a complete break." But another time TR clenched his fist and exclaimed to his cousin Franklin, "Sometimes I wish I could be President and Congress too!" Even patient Lincoln got mad at Congress: "I will show them at the other end of the Avenue whether I am President or not!" And cool John Kennedy opined that "it is much easier in many ways for me—and for other Presidents, I think, who felt the same way—when Congress is not in town."

A wag has said that Congress is composed of representatives running for re-election and Senators running for God. John Adams would have agreed:

But is not man, in the shape of a senator or a representative, as fond of power as a president? . . . are not ambition and favoritism, and all other vicious passions and sinister interests, as strong and active in a senator or a representative as in a president? Cannot, indeed, the members of the legislature conceal their private views and improper motives more easily than a president?

Perhaps. But they are, most of them, honorable men and women, as honor goes in politics, which is a good deal farther than it goes in most endeavors. The President who wants to make the relationship work has to begin with the assumption that their intentions are at least as good as his are, and that they share allegiance to the democratic politician's code: let your word be your bond; fight hard and make up quickly; stick by your friends and be civil with your opponents; listen in the cacophony for strains of agreement; do your homework; and if you can, let everyone have one piece of cake. He learns that the best fringe benefit in politics is the benefit of the doubt, which has a way of coming back to the giver.

Congress used to be a revolving door: members met in short sessions, debated at length, and yearned to get back home and stay there. Nowadays, the sessions are nearly continuous, general debate is rare and relatively meaningless compared to committee work, and a member can make a long career at comfortable pay. Congress is elaborately organized. It seems that nearly everyone is chairman of something. Simplifying reforms, such as cutting down a forest of standing committees, gave growth to scores of subcommittees, which spring up like saplings in the sunshine. Congress is getting its own bureaucracy, its own computers,

Presidential advisers may include political opponents. General Eisenhower went to the White House in June of 1952 to brief Harry Truman on European defenses. Later that week, Eisenhower announced he would seek the GOP nomination for President.

even its own polling capacity. The whole thing is vastly more complicated than when Jefferson dealt with thirty-two senators and 106 representatives. The pecking orders run up, down, and sideways, though those who handle the money—the legislature's most ancient prerogative—are usually at the top of the heap. Party organization is fluid and fragile, the minority too small to hope for much, the majority too large to control easily.

No wonder then that Presidents, particularly those coming in from out of town, need help in discovering and moving the Congressional power levers. The key to it is probably not in the mechanics—how many breakfasts with whom—but in the quality and continuity of the conversation. Genuine, regular consultation is the art to master.

Advisers: Secrecy and Mistakes

The President can expect with confidence at least one kind of counsel from Congress: "Congressmen are always advising Presidents to get rid of Presidential advisers," John Kennedy said. "That's one of the most constant threads that run through American history, and Presidents ordinarily do not pay attention." In just forty years, the White House staff has grown from thirty-seven to more than five hundred, and the "Executive Office of the President" to thousands, circles upon circles. In practical terms, however large his "personal" staff, only forty or so can sustain the coveted claim of intimacy, since the President has only two ears and two eyes and no way to be two places at once. What concerns Congressmen and other thoughtful critics are the dangers of secrecy and mistakes.

What his critics see as secrecy the President sees as privacy. No President so far has managed to get along without private discussion. At the bare minimum, Presidents cannot go public with, say, where the hydrogen bombs are tonight. But even in his day-to-day decision making, the President needs—in the interest of all of us—talk we are not privy to. Candor is in short supply; Presidents suffer from aides hell-bent on "helping" him by nodding to his every pronouncement. He not only needs nay-sayers (ones he can't typecast as certified devil's advocates and then dismiss), he also needs independent souls whose lives would not be over if they no longer worked in the White House. And they have to be—and feel—free to bat around all sorts of damn fool ideas in case one turns out to be viable after all. That is hard to do on television.

Most people understand that. We want open covenants; we don't care too much how they are arrived at. The secrecy that hurts is secrecy about what the President is *doing*—secret wars, secret peace agreements, secret money, secret police. Let him talk to whomever; just keep us informed of the upshots.

Every President ought to have a crony or two, some old boy or girl he can unwind with, play golf, shoot craps, whatever suits his style this side of decency. Cronies' influence always gets exaggerated in the grocery-store press, as if the old friend were Mesmer the hypnotist or

The role allotted the Presidential counselors varies greatly. Few advisers attained the power of Col. Edward House, whom Woodrow Wilson called "my second personality." But near the end of the First World War, as Wilson's physical and mental health declined, he grew suspicious of House, and after Versailles, refused to see him again. The two are pictured here in 1917.

some mind-bending Rasputin. Surely the public's need to know stops short of prying apart those easy bonds. And we might try to leave a President's children in peace, beyond the range of the camera's bug-eyed prurience.

A more serious danger in President-adviser relations is the danger of mistakes with dreadful consequences. Close historical research from a psychological perspective reveals a weird tendency—"groupthink"—for the little knot of advisers around the President to get carried away and to carry him away with them, particularly in crisis circumstances. Psychologists have known for a long time that people in groups will do the strangest things, things they would never do on their own, such as disbelieve their senses or violate their strongest values. A series of cases, including the Bay of Pigs fiasco, shows how the President and his group puffed themselves up into a sense of invulnerability, silenced reasonable doubts, grossly underestimated the opposition, celebrated their fundamentally unexamined unanimity—and were off and running toward disaster.

I think the problem there is isolation, not secrecy. The group locks itself in, locks other counselors out. The risk of leaks is worth taking in such cases, compared to the risk of groupthink. Certainly it makes sense to mix up the group's composition a bit to get some fresh vision. But only the President himself can see to that—call in the Cabinet or the key Congressmen or a maverick or so. And only the President can establish an atmosphere that blends trust and caution, confidence and skepticism, in reasonable proportions to encourage creative conflict.

Chester Cooper, who worked with a President not enthusiastic about dissent, tells how his mind would fog over with groupthink:

During the process I would frequently fall into a Walter Mitty-like fantasy: When my turn came, I would rise to my feet slowly, look around the room and then directly at the President, and say very quietly and emphatically, 'Mr. President, gentlemen, I most definitely do not agree.' But I was removed from my trance when I heard the President's voice saying, 'Mr. Cooper, do you agree?' And out would come a 'Yes, Mr. President, I agree.'

There have been times when Presidents faced too much conflict in the inner circle; Lincoln's Cabinet would qualify as an example, and that problem could arise again. But the modern worry is galloping consensus in the Oval Office.

Bureaucrats and Judges: Compounded Complexity

In the buildings up and down the street from the White House, action consensus is not the danger. In gross terms, the federal bureaucracy has not grown all that much lately (the big growth is in state and city bureaucracies), but parts of it have. The National Security Council staff, for example, a mere fraction of the White House establishment, recently exceeded in number Franklin Roosevelt's entire White House staff—

The modern American President is one of the most powerful figures on the world stage. During World War II, only two months before his death in April, 1945, Franklin Roosevelt met with Churchill and Stalin at Yalta to urge Russia's entry into the war against Japan, and to deal with questions of postwar occupation. Behind them, from left, are British Foreign Minister Anthony Eden, U. S. Secretary of State Edward Stettinius, British Undersecretary Sir Alexander Cadogan, U.S.S.R. Foreign Commissar Vyacheslav Molotov, and U.S. Ambassador Averell Harriman.

experts, executives, secretaries, cooks, bakers, gardeners, and all—at the time World War II was going full blast. The sheer mass of the administrative apparatus has a way of diluting action, muting the Presidential thunder.

Complexity adds more trouble. FDR fumed at the "higgledy-piggledy patchwork of duplicate responsibilities and overlapping powers" he encountered, as had Presidents from Lincoln on. John F. Kennedy was amazed and angered to learn, in the midst of the Cuban missile crisis, that his order to negotiate American missiles out of Turkey—an order issued eighteen months previously—had never been executed. It had run out of steam in the bureaucratic pipeline.

Bureaucrats are just people, honorable men and women again, workers who hope to make a contribution. But organizationally they comprise a collection such as must be somewhere in the Patent Office—inventions old and new, active and moribund, propping each other up with paper. Old agencies die hard, long after their functions pass away. New ones proliferate like kudzu in the rainy season. The reasons are not terribly obscure: give a man a pencil and a desk and he is going to do something. Pretty soon you'll need another man to coordinate him. A committee might help. A liaison person. An executive director. A press office and a grievance office and a legal office and so on. The list of people who have in effect, veto power over the vigorous pursuit of policy stretches down the page, and the odds of policy survival drop off.

A President can grasp this bushel of nettles at one or another handle. All try reorganization in the good old American hope that hooking up the pipes differently might make the water run. Sometimes yes, sometimes no. All times, reforms in the name of simplicity generate new complexities the reformers neglected to imagine. Along the way, though, the reorganizer tends to get some of his people better positioned, and that may help push some progress through the system.

The other handle is inspiration. Kennedy understood the bureaucracy's tired blood problem and dosed it with New Frontierism—the excitement that can lay hold of the hearts of people when hope occurs. Washington filled up with bright young things and great expectations. In the halls of the bureaucracy, many a pointy-headed drone turned himself into a Camelotian go-getter fired with lust for achievement. In hindsight we can see that the results were mixed; some achieved all too well. Lincoln said, "I cannot run this thing upon the theory that every officeholder must think I am the greatest man in the nation, and I will not." But alternatives to chart-shuffling and idealistic dramatics are dim in the minds of the responsible imaginers.

Bureaucracy is meant to help the President get the laws executed. At least since Hammurabi, laws have needed explaining as to what they mean. In a pretty little mausoleum on Capitol Hill sit the nine Solomons of the Supreme Court, the only Federal officers with unlimited tenure, who, figuratively speaking, kiss the President goodbye the day their appointments go through the Senate. Normally he has little to do with them, but he feels their eyes on the back of his neck. Not only can they stay his hand or take his tapes: they symbolize The Law, the whole idea that our common life will run by written rules fairly applied, the primeval idea of our political civilization, God's gift to the Hebrew children. The Supreme Court has a better reputation than the Presidency these days. Not even Roosevelt's mighty win in 1936 could hold back the popular wrath when he trifled with the Court. They have no battalions, only legitimacy. The number of specific Presidential moves they disallow is less significant than the fact, in the President's mind, that if they will, they can.

Peace and Persuasion: Getting with the People

The law's writ, with an exception or two, runs to the water's edge. Beyond is a lawless world, jerry-built from the scraps of a battered sense of humanity, dotted with tin-can dictators and cutthroat terrorists, short on food and shorter on the hope of peace, bullied by gigantic tyrannies too frightened to open up their gates, a world at a loss for what to do with itself. The man I hired will have to look after it, that most powerful man in all the world.

In the end, what does his power amount to? If he has to shoot off the rockets we are all done for, so that's no power. Here at home, he soon discovers by how far his reach exceeds his grasp, that his so-called powers amount to little more than the chance to wheedle in the ears of the other politicians. But with a little bit of luck, he might get through by persuasion, might understand what Erasmus meant when he wrote that "it is no great feat to burn a little man. It is a wonderful achievement to persuade him." And who knows? If the rest of us were to shoulder our civic responsibilities for a change, he might wind up as President, not only of, by, and for the people, but with us.

The President: symbol of power and symbol of the people. Here John Kennedy greets an admiring crowd.

PRESIDENT JIMMY CARTER

I. From boyhood on a red-dirt farm to the governorship of Georgia

by ALEX HALEY

In February, 1932, the farmers in southwest Georgia were finishing the first plowing. Afterward the land would be harrowed and the broken cotton stalks and clumps of Bermuda grass dragged to the edge of the fields and set afire. Then, the turning plows would create endless fields of reddish earth rows, each row enriched with an inch-width of white, coarsely powdered guano fertilizer. Corn would be planted in early March, then the cotton and the other crops. Around Archery and Plains in Sumter County, the principal crop was peanuts.

Before the first plants even peeped above the earth, seven-year-old Jimmy Carter was taking part in an all-out effort to beat down the rampant Bermuda grass. As soon as Jimmy had turned five his daddy, Earl Carter, put him to toting a bucket of drinking water among the family's black tenants, who chopped at the grass with long hoes from daylight to dark. Not until early June, when the cornstalks got as tall as mules' ears, did there come a brief "lay by" time when the workers got about two weeks to rest. Returning to the fields they scythed the ripened grain, then they picked watermelons and hauled them to the Seaboard railroad cars that would take them up North. Then came the first massive cotton picking. Finally, everyone harvested the peanuts, deftly jerking the vines from the earth, with each set of roots holding between thirty and fifty of the plump, light tan nuts, and the vines were stacked so that the nuts could dry in the sun.

Each Saturday morning, now, Jimmy would be out in the nearest field before sunrise. Filling two large buckets with choice peanuts, he would wash them and then boil them in salty water while he rushed through his regular morning chores: he fed the chickens, gathered the eggs, milked a cow, chopped some stovewood and pumped some water

President Jimmy Carter: the official portrait by Charles Rafshoon

for his mother, Lillian, who by then would be cooking breakfast before leaving for her job as a registered nurse. Packing his peanuts into sacks and then into two large picnic baskets, Jimmy would trudge to Plains with that load, about three miles along the railroad track.

Jimmy sold the boiled peanuts for a nickel a bag, up and down the main street of Plains. The Saturday crowd, averaging three hundred or even four hundred farm people, circulated or chitchatted, or played checkers. The aroma of barbecue and cut watermelons was usually in the air, along with small biting flies that made people slap suddenly at their necks or arms, and made the mules—hitched among the wagons, carts and T-model Fords—snort, stomp, swish their tails and shudder their skins. Jimmy would thank each customer, flashing his toothy grin. He might also treat himself to a triple-dip ice cream cone or two, and store-bought candy, and if he had time he would rip and run with some of his schoolmates who lived in town. Sometimes, he would ride on the three-car Seaboard mail train the ten miles to Americus, Georgia, where he would buy a nickel ticket at the Rylander Theater and see a movie.

Around Plains, where everyone had a mental file about everyone else, Earl and Lillian Carter's boy already had a reputation for being feisty and industrious. With eyes blazing and fists flying he had gone after a much larger schoolmate whose rough playing had caused Jimmy's sister Gloria to break her arm. On the other hand, when Gloria hit Jimmy with a wrench, he seized his BB gun and plinked her in the behind. Annoyed one night by the noise of a party his parents were giving, he left his bedroom to sleep in his treehouse, then refused to answer when he was called around midnight, thereby earning himself a memorable switching in the morning.

When Jimmy was nine years old, the Depression was at its lowest point. People around Plains had nothing to eat but what they could grow and catch. Having heard his father swearing that the whole country was going under unless crop prices improved—cotton was then a nickel a pound, peanuts a penny—Jimmy asked permission to invest his savings in five bales of cotton.

Not so many white playmates lived near the Carter farm, so Jimmy played mostly with black boys, some of whose parents were tenants or sharecroppers on Earl Carter's farm. His favorite playmate was A.D. Davis. As soon as they could convince the black foreman, Uncle Jack Clark, that they had done enough work, Jimmy and A.D. would take off, both barefooted, usually with Jimmy's bulldog Bozo. They rolled their barrel hoops down the reddish roads, or shucked off their pants and skinny-dipped in various small ponds near the Carter farm. Or they'd sit on old disc plow blades to go sliding down slick hillocks of pinestraw. The kites they made and flew had long tails festooned with squirming June bugs. They made aerial spinners of corncobs and rooster tail feathers; got stung digging honey from bee trees; harvested wild berries, persimmons, plums and sassafras; dammed up small streams with sticks and red clay; stole rides on Earl Carter's prized bull calf.

One day they went to Americus, where Jimmy insisted they see the

Jim Jack Gordy, above, Lillian's father and Jimmy's grandfather. James Earl Carter, below in army uniform in World War I, was a farmer, Georgia born. The photographs are from the Carter family album.

movie at the Rylander Theater and that A.D. sit with him downstairs in the white-only section. But as a muttering arose, A.D. slipped upstairs to the "crow's nest" followed by Jimmy demanding that he come back downstairs. But A.D. wouldn't and they both left, highly indignant. They found themselves sometimes involved now in embarrassed, confused conversations about race. "Don't know as I'm ever going to start calling you 'Mr. Jimmy,' " said A.D., and Jimmy replied, "I wouldn't blame you—I wouldn't either."

As he grew older, Jimmy began to spend a lot more of his time in Plains. He teamed up with his cousin Hugh Carter and sold hamburgers and ice cream, as well as old newspapers, scrap iron and pennywinkle grubs, which make good fishing bait. The Depression was lifting now, and when the price of cotton went to eighteen cents a pound, Jimmy sold his five nickel-a-pound bales and bought five tenant shacks. Soon he was collecting $16.50 a month in rents—and evoking much headwagging in Plains, where people could tell that Jimmy had inherited his father's business instincts.

About this time Earl Carter opened a new kind of business in Plains. Instead of every farmer hauling peanuts to the oil mill, Carter would pay the best market prices for each man's harvest and sell to the oil mill in wholesale quantities. Business soon expanded to the credit sales of fertilizer, seeds and other supplies. Young Jimmy saw his father bent over his credit ledgers for hours on end.

Frequently now, Jimmy would go thumbing for the thousandth time through his Naval Academy catalogue. He and his father hoped that he would get an appointment to Annapolis, but he worried about the tough physical and academic entrance examinations. He determined to put on more weight. He studied calculus. After Pearl Harbor, Jimmy spent a year at Georgia Southwestern College, then went on to Georgia Tech in Atlanta before enrolling at the Naval Academy in 1943.

Nothing in the catalogue prepared Jimmy for the hazing that the annual crop of plebes was subjected to. Plebe Carter endured his normal share of hazing until one day he refused an upper-classman's order to sing "Marching Through Georgia"—and the rest of his first year became a pure hell. Called a Cracker, often denied food, knocked sprawling with huge serving platters, regularly paddled with long-handled serving spoons, he never did sing General Sherman's song.

That plebe year behind him at last, Midshipman Carter achieved outstanding scholastic averages in gunnery, seamanship, navigation, astronomy, naval tactics and Spanish. He took ballroom dancing, participated in cross-country races and in intercompany football. He learned to fly seaplanes, and of course he learned to be a seaman.

Each summer's training cruise was followed by a brief vacation, and after his junior year Jimmy went home to Plains. One afternoon with but two remaining days at home, his sister Ruth appeared with her friend, Rosalynn Smith, whom Jimmy had known much of his life without giving much thought to her; she was younger, his sister's friend.

Yet that evening he invited her to go to a movie with Ruth and her

Earl Carter, above, with his three eldest children: Jimmy, 7, Gloria, 5, and Ruth, 2. Below, Earl and Lillian Gordy Carter in 1950.

boyfriend, and later that night Jimmy astounded his mother as much as himself by announcing, "Rosalynn's the girl I want to marry."

He lay in his room that night reviewing everything that he—and everyone else in Plains—knew about Rosalynn. The oldest of four children, she had been thirteen when leukemia killed her father, the town mechanic; Rosalynn was helping her mother raise the three younger children. The townspeople respected Rosalynn's strength, stability and self-reliance as well as her thrift and religious devotion. At eighteen she completed a two-year general diploma course at Georgia Southwestern Junior College.

The next night she saw him off as he caught the train to Annapolis. They wrote to each other daily, and they were together when he returned home for Christmas—but she refused his proposal of marriage. Then visiting him at Annapolis two months later, Rosalynn changed her mind. The wedding date was set to follow his graduation in June, 1946.

After the simple ceremony in the packed Plains church, Ensign and Mrs. Carter settled down in a small apartment in Norfolk, Virginia, where he had been assigned to the battleship *Wyoming*. He was reassigned to the *Mississippi*. In July, 1947, their son was born, named John William but called "Jack." Though the navy life was more exciting than anything they had ever known in their tiny, dusty, Georgia hometown, it was frustrating with his ship so often and so long at sea. Hoping to get them more time together somehow, Jimmy applied for a Rhodes scholarship; the request was turned down, but he was accepted for submarine officers' training in New London, Connecticut.

He finished third among fifty-two classmates, drawing a submarine assignment — U.S.S. *Pomfret* — that would send the Carters to Oahu, Hawaii, for the next four years. When Jimmy was home, they loved packing a picnic hamper and strolling barefoot on the beach with Jack scampering before them, filling his pail with multi-colored seashells, and suddenly rushing ahead, squealing with delight as his presence sent little armies of walnut-sized sandcrabs fleeing. Caring for Jack alone when Jimmy was away, Rosalynn sewed and sometimes shared coffee chitchat with other submariners' wives—who later described her as a "shy" and "very private" person—and she read more books than she once

Main Street, Plains, Georgia, opposite, still looks much as it did in 1925 when this picture was made. The general supply store, left, that Earl Carter ran until 1928 is at the far left of the street.

would have thought existed. She became pregnant again and a second son, James Earl, was born, whom the hospital nurses nicknamed "Chip."

The *Pomfret* was reassigned to San Diego in 1950 and Carter was ordered to New London as senior officer of the pre-commissioning detail of the first new ship built by the navy since the end of World War II, *K-1*, a small submarine designed to fight submerged enemy vessels. He supervised the *K-1's* construction, the installing of special sonar equipment, and developed operating procedures to be used on the ship.

Carter was not senior enough to have a ship of his own while serving on the *K-1*, though he was qualified to command a submarine. Sometimes, he and the other officers and crew remained submerged for weeks at a time in the small sub, testing the sophisticated underwater listening equipment. Once, a crewman went mad with claustrophobia and had to be strapped to a bunk until the *K-1* could surface and he could be taken away by helicopter to a hospital. It was not easy duty. But Carter and his fellow submariners felt a great personal closeness, proud of being part of such a demanding service and of the high standards required. When Carter heard that Admiral Hyman Rickover had persuaded the navy to begin a nuclear submarine program, he applied at once to become part of such a challenging assignment. This returned them to New London, where a third son, Jeffrey, was born soon after they arrived. Carter and three other young officers were sent to Schenectady, New York, to oversee the developing prototype nuclear submarine, *Sea Wolf*. By day the lieutenant taught his prospective crewmen physics, math and the ABC's of nuclear reactors. He attended Union College to study atomic science and technology. The fact that he had managed to qualify for this handpicked nuclear submarine post at the age of twenty-eight pointed him on a straight course to an eventual nuclear admiralty.

But then came a phone call from Plains; Earl Carter was dying with inoperable cancer. Jimmy and his family drove 1,100 miles nearly non-stop to return home, and once there he plunged into work at the family warehouse, trying his best to be a substitute for his father. From one customer after another, he heard stories of how in troubled times "just about everybody" had come to Earl Carter, who had lent cash and extended substantial credit when no bank would, later even canceling out

Jimmy, not yet a year old, with his cousin Hugh, above; below, at 5 with 3-year-old Gloria.

some of the debts—demanding only that none of his family be told.

In the early evenings Jimmy sat at his father's bedside. Since Jimmy had grown up and left home, they had on occasion gotten into harsh arguments on social and political issues. But now his stricken father lay thanking his son for coming, telling him how proudly he had followed Jimmy's navy career.

When Earl Carter died, Jimmy and his sister Ruth went driving along the red clay roads around Plains, breaking the news to white and black, many of whom burst into tears. At the funeral, mourners filled even the yard of the Plains Baptist Church.

When it was over, Jimmy and Rosalynn returned to Schenectady, and he began to brood. It was a while before he could bring himself to share his anguish even with Rosalynn. His father had been a mainstay, a caretaker of their community, he told her. Who else now could fill his father's place? Rosalynn understood Jimmy's feelings, but she also knew that she must not permit her husband to wreck his brilliant career, his years of disciplined studying. And she wondered if they could ever be content to live again in Plains. The worst arguments they'd had before had generally been solved quickly, but this time it was different. His determination to return brought out a similarly fierce determination in Rosalynn, but when she sensed that she might be wrecking their marriage, she gave in.

Back in Plains, they moved into a $30-a-month apartment in the Plains public housing project. Rosalynn would look at him at times wondering to herself what kind of man would jettison a brilliant, secure career to return to tiny, dusty Plains and raise peanuts. Returning late each night, he kept her posted on the family's financial state of affairs. Earl Carter had left some cash, most of which went to taxes, and some land, and the accounts receivable—the total of outright cash loans and supplies he had issued on credit to scores of local farmers. One worry was how many of the creditors might simply abandon the dead man's debts. But even those who planned to pay the Carters back couldn't do so without a reasonable harvest, and the outlook was for a drought.

Rosalynn began going to the warehouse, studying the books closely. Soon she plunged in more deeply and worked her way through a good course in professional accounting. Though the family was existing on savings bonds, Jimmy had the habit of arriving for lunch with some uninvited guest. So they shared Rosalynn's homemade chicken soup, stews, and casseroles with a succession of county agents and farmers whose brains her husband was eagerly and candidly picking. He had to get re-oriented, he told Rosalynn, and learn about the revolutionary new agriculture techniques, machines and chemicals that had turned farming into a science: hardly a hand-plow or working mule could now be found in Sumter County.

The 1954 drought was far worse than had been expected. Weekday after weekday only a trickle of wagons arrived at the warehouse, loaded with generally runty peanuts. With the nearly record poor harvest, few warehouse debts got paid. Over and over again in the small office,

Rosalynn heard her husband telling their customers, "Of course, I under-stand." Her final accounting showed their year's net profit to be $254.

One day in the early spring of 1955, the Plains police chief dropped by the warehouse accompanied by a Baptist preacher who also served as the railroad depot agent. They were forming a local chapter of the White Citizens Council, and they asked him to join. Jimmy refused. They left abruptly wearing set, flushed faces. Before long the two men returned accompanied by some of the warehouse's few cash customers, one of whom explained to Jimmy that he was risking his personal reputation and his family's business if he still refused to join. Jimmy told them that he had no intention of joining; if necessary, he decided, he and his family would leave Plains. Overnight, most of their customers vanished. Worst of all, some people in the congregation whom they had known all their lives stopped speaking to them. Gradually, though, the customers began to return. It had gone around the grapevine that Jimmy's naval career had warped him, but that now he'd come around.

He didn't. After efforts to integrate a white Baptist church in Americus created a furor there, the Plains Baptist Church proposed to bar all blacks or civil rights workers; only Jimmy, Rosalynn and Lillian Carter, and Jeffrey and Chip Carter and one other member of the entire congregation voted no, against fifty yea's. Again many quit speaking to the dissident Carters. Even so, the people of Plains had deep respect for honest dealing and hard work, and it was commonly agreed that there wasn't a smarter young couple in town than Jimmy and Rosalynn Carter.

Rosalynn was painfully shy, but she had the trust of the farmers when "settling up" time came. Jimmy boasted to customers that in addition to being his wife, Rosalynn had become his indispensable busi-ness partner. By the late fifties, they had installed more than $100,000 worth of peanut-hulling machinery. And in 1960, Rosalynn showed Jimmy her careful figures that indicated they really could afford to build the house they wanted; the next year the five of them moved into their new ranch-style house of Georgia clay red bricks.

One day in 1962, Jimmy told Rosalynn that the Georgia legislature was being reapportioned and that he still had time to file for the state senate. His campaign was most notable for its feverishness, but when election day finally came he got the shock of his life. At one polling place in Quitman County, voters were marking their ballots in full view of the local political boss, who was telling them to vote for Carter's op-ponent. The man was even taking the ballots out of the pasteboard box and examining them.

Thus Carter began to learn an infuriating lesson about the capaci-ties of corrupt politicians to cover up their crookedness. Eventually, reporter John Pennington of the *Atlanta Journal* published an exposé of Quitman County politics that led to a formal court action. The prosecu-tion showed that the county voting register included the names of the departed, the dead, and the imprisoned. The court ordered a new election and Jimmy Carter won by 1500 votes.

Senator Carter served two terms that spanned a period when race

Young Jimmy above with ponies and below with his dog Bozo.

had become the most incendiary topic in Southern politics. Jimmy had a few colleagues who were not content to accept the bitter irrationalities they heard from older legislators. The young senators agreed that the traditional social order could hardly be changed overnight, but that there were a few decent things they could do to begin changing it. Jimmy himself had come to believe that racial, ethnic and religious prejudice was the most costly flaw in the U.S. fabric—probably the greatest obstacle to our ever realizing our fullest national potential.

Accordingly, Jimmy took a strong stand against Georgia's traditional "thirty questions literacy test"—virtually impossible to pass—which had long been used to keep blacks from voting. That same year, his mother Lillian and sister Gloria volunteered to work in Americus at Lyndon Johnson's election headquarters. Because of his stand on civil rights, Johnson was unpopular in the South. Lillian came out of the headquarters often to find her car smeared with soap, the aerial tied into a knot and threatening messages left on the front seat. Back in Plains, children hurled things at her car and called her "nigger-lover." And Chip Carter was beaten up at school for wearing an "LBJ" button.

By this time, Miss Lillian was thinking of widening her own horizons. In 1964 she had gone to the Democratic National Convention, then joined a goodwill tour of the Soviet Union and eastern Europe for the State Department. "They were rewarding experiences," she said, "but over too quick, and soon I was bored again. I'm not a religious fanatic, but I *am* a Christian, and I was certain there was something important I was intended to do."

She found out what that was one spring, and seeking Jimmy and Billy out at the warehouse one afternoon, she asked them if they loved her. Jimmy said, "Of course we do, Mama," but Billy was blunter. "What in hell are you up to now?" So she showed him her application form and told them she had joined the Peace Corps. "Age is no barrier," the television commercial had said, and now, at sixty-eight, she was on her way to Chicago for orientation and then to India, where she was going to be a nurse. Her sons knew better than to try to stop her.

Back on the home front, Jimmy wrote and supported so much legislation for education, mental health, and consumer reform that in his second term, he was named one of Georgia's two outstanding state legislators.

Carter made up his mind to run for Congress from his district, the third district of Georgia. His opponent was to be Howard Callaway, the wealthy, articulate young Republican congressman from the district. They had long been competitors: Callaway led Georgia's Republicans, while Carter was regarded as one of the state's most promising young Democrats; furthermore, Callaway was a West Point man, and he and Annapolis graduate Carter had a certain tendency to bristle at each other. In the late spring of 1966, Jimmy launched a grassroots campaign after the legislature adjourned, making speeches, meeting voters, asking them how they stood on various issues, returning home late each night with a list of names and addresses of the people he had met. He or

Rosalynn Smith, here in a big hairbow and best dress, was a shy little girl whose father was the mechanic in Plains. She and Jimmy paid little attention to each other until they were grown up. *Opposite:* Jimmy, age 7.

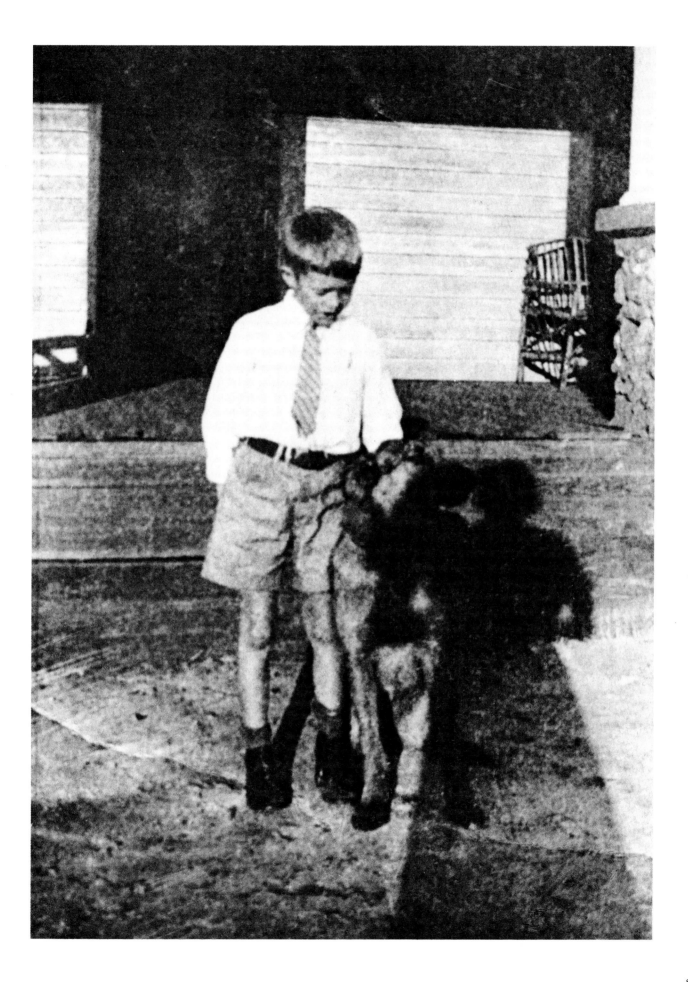

Rosalynn or his sister Gloria wrote notes to them all, asking for their vote.

Callaway announced for governor instead of Congress. Later when the Democratic front runner withdrew from the contest, Carter determined to run for governor himself. Only three months remained before the statewide Democratic primary; he had to win that before he could tackle Callaway in the general election in November. For over two years Callaway had been the daily subject of statewide news stories, while Jimmy was scarcely well known in the same way. "Jimmy *Who?*" he was quickly dubbed by the Atlanta press. But Jimmy thought he could win.

The news of his candidacy gave Georgia Republicans their biggest guffaw in a long time, though it hardly amused Democrats in his home congressional district to see him abandon a campaign that he surely could have won. The first Sunday afternoon that he called his supporters to Atlanta, only a handful appeared. Frantically, he campaigned through Georgia, and gradually those Sunday meetings began to draw more supporters. He *was* making headway, he could see it. Crippled by lack of money and of volunteer workers, he called upon Rosalynn and their sons and they campaigned actively all over the state.

Nearly 800,000 voters turned out for the Democratic primary, and Jimmy Carter ran *third*. In forty-two years he had never felt such a crushing sense of disappointment. Deep in debt and thinner than ever, he felt depressed and discouraged.

At church one Sunday Jimmy heard the minister challenge his flock: "If you were arrested for being a Christian, would there be enough evidence to convict you?" Telling Rosalynn how deeply that question left him shaken, he said he felt he needed to go and manifest his faith, and she understood.

He got involved with a missionary program through his church and went to witness for his faith in Pennsylvania and Massachusetts, moving among people, knocking at their doors and greeting them. Jimmy would tell them, "I'm a farmer from Georgia," and talk quietly of his Christian beliefs. When he returned, Rosalynn had news he had not expected to hear again: she had just learned that she was pregnant.

The inner peace he had regained as a witness for his faith, and as the prospective father of a new baby, had renewed his strength, his energy—and his determination to win the governorship. In the course of the next three weeks, he planned a gubernatorial campaign plan so thorough in its statewide coverage and with such infiltration among all voters that he could not see how it could possibly fail.

He reviewed his list of campaign volunteers and soon set them to the task of collecting, organizing and then actually memorizing what grew within days into a Georgia-wide atlas of county maps. They made an exhaustive study of the previous voting patterns within each county. The results were a code of varicolored plastic tabs and stick pins arranged demographically upon each county's map.

In the midst of all this Rosalynn—at forty—delivered a perfect baby girl whom they called Amy. "She makes me feel I'm starting young all over again!" Jimmy exclaimed.

Midshipman Carter. He chose Annapolis partly out of admiration for an uncle who was in the navy, partly because times were hard and he needed the free education.

Redoubling his zeal, Jimmy organized an eight-county commission to study the techniques of long-range planning and development. Then the commission was expanded state-wide with him as its first state president. With that platform, he knew he could go anywhere in Georgia, speaking and campaigning, and he did just that. Nor was that enough; as a longstanding member of the Plains Lions Club, he became state chairman of the six regional districts containing the 180 Lions Clubs. In small towns like Plains these were the focal point for nearly all political and civic activities. Already prominent in religious and agricultural organizations, he became an official in the statewide March of Dimes.

"Show me a good loser and I'll show you a loser. I do not intend to lose again!" he pledged to his volunteers. No city or town or hamlet escaped hearing about Senator Jimmy Carter. Rising before dawn, he had his day's plan on paper by breakfast time. For the rest of the morning he worked at the warehouse, and then after lunch drove away, speaking to sometimes as many as three groups. On the way home he dictated politically useful information into a tape recorder, knowing that Rosalynn would transcribe and file it and write brief notes when necessary. He sometimes found it difficult to believe that the formidable woman who had become the keel of his life had once been the shy nineteen-year-old he had married. He thought that no woman could be any more dependable and direct and firm; yet with their children, and in their own private times together, neither could any woman possibly have been more dear, and sweet, and tender.

With the next primary election's date looming a year ahead, Jimmy

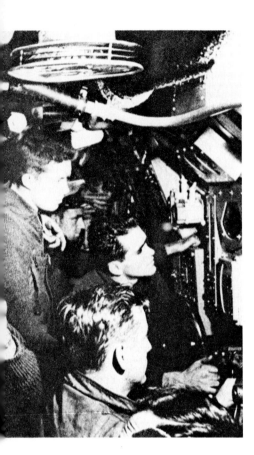

cranked his campaign into high gear. Guided by his color-coded findings posted upon large charts and graphs, he and his family and his staff blanketed the state. They did not, as a rule, stay in hotels or motels, but in the homes of local supporters, both to save money and to get people involved.

As the 1970 primary drew nearer, he was more committed than ever and so was Rosalynn. Jimmy had told her he needed her help on the campaign trail not only as his companion but as a speaker on her own. Rosalynn was at first fearful she'd be a liability. But she tried, because Jimmy had asked her to. He had no idea what a giant step it represented to her. "It was the hardest thing I'd ever had to do in my life," she admitted later. But after the first ordeal or two, campaigning was almost effortless for Rosalynn. She and Jimmy met workers at the factory gates, pumped hands in department stores, went into beauty shops, barber shops, restaurants, gas stations, school picnics, rodeos, livestock shows.

The staff, the candidate and his family were exhausted as they moved into the final week of the campaign. Carter had proved himself one of the most driving, driven, relentless campaigners the South had ever seen. He alone had made nearly 1,800 speeches; he and Rosalynn had shaken hands with some 600,000 people—more than half of the eligible voters in Georgia. The day of the 1970 gubernatorial election at last arrived and he won it, big.

Calling Georgia's administrative organization "a tangle of overlapping civil service bureaucracies and patronage fiefs dating back forty years," promising its massive reorganization, he set about borrowing 100 management experts from industry, government and universities. Their resulting 300 recommendations evoked a howling din of protests while a reorganization program was written. He fought it through the legislature, then in such a grueling senate battle that it was at last by a single vote that he won the radical consolidation of government functions into only twenty-two agencies.

Next challenging the fiscal crisis with what he termed "zero-based budgeting," Governor Carter required every department head to justify each annual dollar spent for his programs. Among the other efforts and achievements of his one-term administration, he raised the number of significant black state appointees from three to fifty-three; opened the government meaningfully to women; formed a commission for land preservations; vigorously fought air and water pollution; took steps to humanize care for the mentally disturbed; improved prison conditions; organized Georgia's first narcotic-addiction centers; fought for tough consumer-protection laws and new banking regulations; spearheaded new programs in the area of health care and education; constantly traveled the state listening to citizen complaints—and acting on them.

Rough even on his own staff, he was sometimes stern about responsibility, efficiency, punctuality, brevity. He rejected memos over three pages long, unless they were of the greatest importance. He never wanted to hear anyone give him reasons why anything couldn't be done. In conferences, he generated conflicts. He listened intently even to heretical

advice on any issue. Then he considered what he had heard with what his own knowledge and beliefs and intuitions said, and he made up his mind. Once having done that, he was not apt to change it, ever. Said one of his oldest, closest friends, Georgia Secretary of State Ben Fortson, "He's stubborn as a south Georgia turtle."

On February 17, 1974, Carter made Georgia history by hanging portraits of Martin Luther King, Jr. and two other distinguished black Georgians in the state house. Yet, perhaps as memorable as anything during his term was the inaugural speech of the state of Georgia's seventy-sixth governor. It surprised and even shocked a great many people, but it is well worth quoting now: *Our people are our most precious possession. We cannot afford to waste the talents and abilities given by God to one single person. Every adult illiterate, every school dropout, every untrained retarded child is an indictment of us all. Our state pays a terrible and continuing price for these failures. I say to you quite frankly that the time for racial discrimination is over. No poor, rural, weak or black person should ever have to bear the additional burden of being deprived of the opportunity of an education, a job, or simple justice.*

That the man who spoke those words in the state of Georgia scarcely seven brief years ago has come to the high office he has just assumed is surely one of the most amazing political events of our times. In recent

Carter's first submarine duty was on the U.S.S. *Pomfret,* above. He is second from left. Opposite, on board the U.S.S. *K-1*, with Carter standing at left. Later he worked in the nuclear submarine program at New London, Connecticut, but resigned from the navy and returned home after Earl Carter's death in 1953.

years it has sometimes seemed to the American people as if power goes mainly to the powerful, wealth to those that have no need of it, education to the sons and daughters of the educated. And the old hope that any child might grow up to be President has come to seem a little foolish. Not since the nineteenth century has a Southerner and farmer come to the White House. Knowing, as he does know, that it hurts to be on the losing side, he can, we trust, restore us to our faith that people *are* the most precious possession of this nation, and that each child and each man and each woman matters, whether black or white.

II. How Carter came to the Presidency: a new kind of campaign

by HAL GULLIVER

It was a cold, clear night in Iowa nearly a full year before the Presidential election, the snow from the day before still on the ground. The candidate asked a local radio reporter to ride back out to the airport with him after the last stop of that particularly long campaign day.

The reporter wanted to tape an interview, and though the candidate had answered many of the same questions a dozen times that day, he answered them again patiently. He even seemed to enjoy it, especially when the reporter asked a hard follow-up question. Indeed, the candidate had often campaigned in Iowa before and had been interviewed more than once by this same reporter, a young college student who was working at the local radio station.

As the car neared the airport, the candidate turned the tables and began to interview the reporter a little. What would the young man do when he finished college? Go on working in radio? The reporter wasn't sure. It was more than a year before he would finish college, he said. "Well," the candidate replied, "by that time I expect to be President of the United States and if you still have not made up your mind maybe you could come by the White House for a visit and talk about future plans."

The candidate's small rented plane was tuning up, ready for the flight back to Des Moines, and he said good-bye. The young reporter had a curious, quiet, bemused expression on his face.

Even earlier, eighteen months before the Presidential election, the candidate was campaigning in Philadelphia, where he stayed overnight with some friends who had recently moved there from Atlanta. They were delighted to see him again, but unsure about his political hopes. They were all up early for breakfast, another long campaign day ahead, and the candidate padded around the kitchen in bare feet, fixed himself a cup of coffee, then stopped short in the middle of a conversation, grinned at his two friends and said, "I know you both probably think I'm crazy, but I really think I'm going to be the next President of the United States."

Quail hunting is something Jimmy Carter has enjoyed since he was a boy of 10. Above, he pats his bird dog, and opposite sets off across the fields near Plains.

Returning to Plains, Jimmy and Rosalynn worked together to turn the family farm into a modern, profitable operation. Above, Carter farm machinery. *Opposite:* Announcing his candidacy for governor, 1970, Carter, above left, was interrupted by his daughter Amy. She is with her mother, flanked by her Aunt Ruth and her grandmother. Carter won, succeeding Lester Maddox, who listens to Carter's first budget message, below.

That was a lighter moment. It was during that same early Philadelphia visit, in the winter of 1975, that the candidate suffered what he later called one of the most embarrassing moments of the entire campaign. A staff member had rented a room in a downtown hotel and announced a press conference. The staffer and the candidate were there at the appointed time. No one else came, no one at all.

The candidate of course was James Earl Carter, now the thirty-ninth President, and he would say later that those first months of campaigning over the country, before the national news media began to take him seriously, were in some ways the most interesting of all, a time when he learned a good deal about the concerns of average Americans. He was campaigning among them almost on a one-to-one basis, talking in living rooms and to small groups, answering questions, only rarely being trailed by even a lone radio reporter.

Late in the campaign, Carter would sometimes sit by the window of his huge chartered jet, *Peanut One,* so very different from the small planes of the early days in Iowa, and look down at whatever state was below. He could remember when he last campaigned there, and he would recall, perhaps, that there was good farmland in that part of the state or what the major local industry was, and he knew when his wife Rosalynn had last been there. Carter once observed that he and his wife, his mother Lillian, his three sons and their wives, his sister Ruth and his Aunt Sissy had spent so much time in so many different communities that these experiences, cumulatively, could provide an invaluable help to a President trying really to understand and deal with the problems of more than 220 million people.

Jimmy Carter's formal campaign to win the Presidential nomination and election began officially on Thursday December 12, 1974, as he entered his last month of a four-year term as governor of Georgia.

"I am a farmer, an engineer, a businessman, a planner, a scientist, a governor and a Christian. Each of you is an individual and different from all the others. Yet we Americans have shared one thing in common: a belief in the greatness of our country," said Carter in his formal announcement, as he stated themes that he would restate in the long campaign, that Americans have dared to dream great dreams for this nation, to take seriously the promises of decency and equality and freedom and of an honest and responsible government. "The root of the problem is not so much that our people have lost confidence in government but that government has demonstrated time and again its lack of confidence in the people," Carter declared, asserting that American dreams and ideals still live in our "collective heart" and that the times demand political leadership that will realize those dreams, rather than appealing to doubts and prejudices and fears.

That was the beginning of Carter's formal campaign for the White House. But any national campaign begins informally in a somewhat different way, in that informal moment when the candidate decides to seek the most powerful elective office in the world.

With Jimmy Carter, that process began after his upset election as

governor of Georgia in 1970, as he began increasingly to play a role in national politics. He was active in regional and national governors' conferences, and in the affairs of the national Democratic party, even as he was also working to reorganize the Georgia state government—as he had promised. He also consulted potential Presidential candidates from both major parties, Republicans and Democrats, and began to take an interest in national and international issues.

That informal moment of decision, that decision to make the bid for the White House, came in the late summer of 1972, even before the national election. It seemed clear to Carter and his inner circle that the nation would be ready for new leadership by 1976, and the more they discussed it the more it seemed possible that a Georgia peanut farmer (and nuclear engineer) might be able to offer such leadership.

There were immediate apparent disadvantages.

Carter could not, under the Georgia constitution, succeed himself as governor, and he would have no political base for a national campaign. Moreover, political parties in modern times have looked to the U.S. Senate for Presidential candidates; not one governor or recent ex-governor had been a Presidential candidate in two decades. In addition

Three generations of Carter women: Lillian at Pond House in Plains; Amy on the trampoline behind the governor's mansion in Atlanta; Rosalynn at a rally in New Jersey in October, 1976.

Carter was a farmer—hardly an advantage—from the Deep South, from which no President had come in more than a century. And worse, perhaps, he came from the small town of Plains. Financing would be hard to get, and the national news media are concentrated in Washington and New York—a definite disadvantage for a politically unemployed ex-governor of Georgia.

Yet, curiously, Carter concluded that there were compensating factors. Not everybody looked unfavorably on farmers or on small town origins. If being out of office had a negative side, it also meant that a candidate would have full time to campaign. Money would be a problem, but Carter believed that a small, dedicated staff along with substantial numbers of volunteers could overcome it. National news media do focus on Washington, but a Presidential candidate campaigning early might get excellent state and regional news coverage that in time would add up to national influence. Even being a Southerner had a dual dimension. In 1960 Georgia gave John Kennedy an overwhelming margin of victory, though people had said Southerners would never vote for a Roman Catholic. In 1976 could American voters be persuaded to overcome regional bias as well?

Overleaf: **Madison Square Garden and the Democratic National Convention, July, 1976, where Carter won the first ballot nomination.**

Some nineteen months after he entered the race, "Jimmy Who?" won the nomination. Here at the convention, Carter listens as the Rev. Martin Luther King, Sr., delivers the invocation.

Carter now admits it is true that when he first told his mother, Mrs. Lillian Carter, that he intended to run for President, she asked, "President of what?" But many of Carter's circle in Georgia, in government and out, took these early plans quite seriously, believing that Carter had the intelligence and integrity and capacity to be a good President. They began to move quietly to raise money and to try to be otherwise helpful in a national campaign.

Carter brought two assets to his campaign that have perhaps not been readily understood by political pundits. First, he usually described himself as a "planner," and in his Georgia campaigns and as governor he proved that he was a planner and organizer of the first water. He once remarked that planning a national political campaign seemed almost impossible until, that is, you began to think of each state individually and each congressional district within a state and how to mount an effective campaign in each district. Carter was a master of such details. He could even plan a full year ahead just how many campaign days he should allot to a particular state.

Secondly, Carter is one of the best person-to-person campaigners in modern American history, almost certainly the best since the late Senator Estes Kefauver of Tennessee. One of his severest critics, who at an early stage dismissed Carter's Presidential chances, commented nonetheless that "Jimmy Carter will carry any precinct in which he personally campaigns." But the critic did not believe that Carter could ever get around the country and campaign in enough precincts to be effective.

But that came later, after the formal announcement in late December of 1974. The real decision was made in late 1972, and afterward Carter began to prepare himself not only for a national campaign but for the White House itself. He had routinely read three or four books a week, and now he included more and more volumes on defense and foreign policy and economics. He also began to expand his existing ties within the national Democratic party, assuming in 1973 and 1974 the role of chairman of the Democratic Party Campaign Committee, not necessarily an exciting assignment in an off-Presidential year. Carter worked enthusiastically to inform himself about the thirty-four senatorial campaigns that fall and the thirty-five gubernatorial campaigns and 435 congressional races, putting together a basic package of position papers that might be helpful to Democratic candidates. Then in the fall of 1974 he worked personally with more than sixty candidates and campaigned actively in their behalf.

It was all a "good learning experience," Carter said later, and when it was over he knew the country a good deal better, and had earned the friendship of a number of key Democrats who now knew Jimmy Carter personally.

Yet, the first months of campaigning after the formal announcement were often hard. Carter was the lonely, long distance runner, a Jimmy Who? candidate, a longshot, and even to knowledgeable Democrats, perhaps at best a darkhorse candidate for Vice President. A typical Carter day went from factory shift changes in the early morning through meetings and shopping centers and college campuses, often ending up in the late evening in someone's living room where a supporter had assembled twenty or thirty neighbors to look at the Georgian who wanted to be in the White House.

Those living room sessions were important. Carter would talk of his sense of the country, his vision of America and its past and its future and his conviction that the strengths and ideals of the American people could overcome any current problem. Then he would answer questions on any and everything. Usually, he could give a detailed answer about his own views on any topic, but he learned to say, sometimes, "I just don't know."

The campaign was run with a small staff and volunteers and a shoestring budget. Twice it absolutely ground to a halt, and Carter had to return to Georgia to raise money. But by the end of 1975 the incredible effort extended by Carter and his family, his staff and volunteers, began to pay off. By then Carter had raised enough money in small contribu-

tions from the required twenty states to qualify for the upcoming federal matching money under the new campaign financing law. In Iowa, which held the earliest caucus to select Democratic convention delegates, a *Des Moines Register* poll of state Democrats gave Carter a startling lead. In 1975 Florida Democrats held their first state convention in a century, and an overwhelming sixty-seven percent of the 1,035 state delegates picked Jimmy Carter for President. After Carter spoke at a Florida convention dinner, one prominent national Democrat remarked that he had rarely seen such enthusiasm in a crowd, that there were sparks in the air.

Carter's strategy now became apparent. His first and critical decision, perhaps the most important of his campaign, was to seek delegates everywhere, in all the thirty or so states with either caucuses or primaries. The other candidates were carefully planning to go only into selective primaries, choosing those states where they might have the best chance, reasoning that with so many candidates afield, that a deadlocked convention would eventually move in this direction or that. Carter never believed in that scenario, partly because of his accurate sense of American history; such a deadlock had not occurred since the Democratic convention of 1924, which went more than one hundred ballots. Carter knew that a front runner in the primaries would win the nomination on the first or second ballot.

The second part of Carter's strategy was to focus special attention on three vital states: Iowa, New Hampshire, and Florida. Iowa held its caucus in January. New Hampshire traditionally held the first primary, in late February, and the results there always had national impact. Florida had an early primary too, on March 9, the first Southern primary, which was of special importance for Carter. Any Southern Presidential candidate must show strength in his home region if he wanted to be taken seriously as a national candidate. Moreover, the Florida primary would pit Carter against Governor George Wallace, considered unbeatable after his huge win in the Florida primary in 1972.

Carter devoted more time to grass roots campaigning in these three states—Iowa, New Hampshire, and Florida—than anywhere else. He discovered that, even in New Hampshire, few national candidates had ever campaigned in that fashion. As he noted in his autobiography, *Why Not the Best?,* local workers in Concord and Manchester and state employees in the capital said that they had never actually *seen* a Presidential candidate before.

The impact of that kind of campaigning—and of the careful organization behind it—soon became clear. Carter carried the Iowa caucus with twice as many votes as his closest opponent. He won the New Hampshire primary, over other candidates far better known nationally. On March 9, Carter won the Florida primary, defeating Wallace and others—a feat most pundits had called impossible.

The Georgian's march through the later primaries was sometimes triumphant, though sometimes there were setbacks. North Carolina, Illinois, Wisconsin, and Pennsylvania were significant. Carter's solid win in the Pennsylvania primary in late April was the last hurrah for

No Presidential candidate in recent memory has campaigned more intensively than Carter. Above, the candidate motors through New York City, and at left greets voters in Pennsylvania. Below is an array of campaign ephemera.

the ABC crowd (Anybody But Carter), a temporary coalition who hoped to undercut his momentum. The Super Bowl of the primary season came in early June when California, New Jersey, and Ohio had primaries on the same day; Carter carried Ohio by an enormous margin and picked up substantial numbers of delegates in both New Jersey and California. putting him within reach of the nomination. Governor Wallace and Senator Henry Jackson and Mayor Richard Daley promptly endorsed Carter, and it was over. The long distance runner had made it all the way.

The general election in November was something else again, of course, and Carter warned his supporters at the Democratic convention in New York City that the worst thing they could do was to take voters for granted. The polls showed Carter the going-away favorite to win on November 2nd. But as he predicted, the margin dropped. President Gerald Ford conducted a vigorous campaign and it was clear, as Rosalynn Carter said, that it is hard under any circumstances to defeat an incumbent President.

Victory can claim a thousand fathers, while defeat is an orphan. Many can rightly claim some part in Jimmy Carter's election. But two groups deserve some special mention because of their importance to the campaign and because of their quite early support. Carter, who grew up in the segregated Deep South, drew his sturdiest backing from blacks. Influential black Georgians like Atlanta Congressman Andrew Young and Martin Luther King, Sr. and Coretta King spoke up for him early, and black voters in state after state were solidly for Carter. The second group overlaps the first, made up of Georgians, black and white, who formed the "Peanut Brigades" and who traveled at their own expense to other states and campaigned door to door for their favorite son. Two hundred sixty Georgians once gathered before dawn to take a chartered flight to go campaigning for Jimmy Carter, not knowing even where they were bound. A couple of important states were being considered, and the decision was made shortly before take-off. Georgians unaccustomed to such weather found themselves in the ice and snows of New Hampshire, Wisconsin, and northern New York, as well as in the Florida sun next door.

There was a central perception to Carter's campaign more important than any tactical decision. Carter understood that we wanted to believe in our government and our national ideals, that after Watergate and Vietnam we wanted a sense of purpose and *trust*—trust in our national leaders. Can government be efficient and competent? Can government at the same time be honest and open and decent and compassionate? These were questions Carter asked over and over, saying that many Americans feared the answer to both questions was no. Yet he was convinced the answer could be yes, that the American system of government and the character of the American people had not changed so completely in the past two hundred years.

While Carter was governor he once met the governors of the twelve other original states in Philadelphia, exactly two hundred years after the meeting there of the First Continental Congress. Later Carter wrote

Early in the morning on November 3, Mississippi reported in, and Jimmy and Rosalynn Carter, at their suite in the Omni Hotel in Atlanta, knew they would be the next President and First Lady of the land.

about sitting in Carpenter's Hall in the same chairs in which Samuel Adams and Patrick Henry and George Washington had sat, men of widely differing views who somehow in the end avoided timid compromise resolutions. "They were somehow inspired, and they reached for greatness," he said.

Carter spoke of that experience in December of 1974 when he first announced formally for the White House. Were those early American leaders more competent or intelligent or better educated than Americans today? More courageous? More compassionate? Had they a deeper concern than we about the future, or deeper religious beliefs? "Our government can express the highest common ideals of human beings—*if* we demand of it standards of excellence," Carter declared, asserting that we are as able as our forebears to correct our faults, manage our own affairs, and face the future with confidence.

James Earl Carter of Plains, Georgia, at age fifty-two the thirty-ninth President of the United States, is convinced that as we begin our third century we can indeed demand standards of excellence of ourselves . . . and of our government.

Back in Plains as November 3 dawned, the President-elect spoke of "a new spirit, a new commitment," for America. Rosalynn is beside him.

VICE PRESIDENT WALTER F. MONDALE

The Minnesota heritage of progressivism

Walter "Fritz" Mondale was only ten years old when he first saw the capital of the country he would one day help govern. Unlike the triumphal figure who marched down Pennsylvania Avenue with President Jimmy Carter on Inaugural Day thirty-nine years later, the future Vice President of the United States looked unimpressive when he first came to Washington from Minnesota with his parents and two brothers in July, 1938.

Mondale's family made the 1,100-mile trip from their home in Elmore, Minnesota, in a green 1935 Ford pulling a trailer that his father had made from a flatbed truck. The trailer's plywood sides and roof were painted a shiny aluminum color and it held canned goods, a stove, and beds so the family would not have to pay for food or lodging.

The trip was a success even though the car broke down somewhere in Missouri and the trailer, which had no brakes, proved a constant hazard as it weaved and jerked its way along the road. When the Mondales finally reached Washington, they parked at a campground on Hains Point and, looking like a family fleeing the dust bowl in search of a new life, went directly to the Capitol. There, they were greeted by the elder Mondale's favorite senator, white-haired Henrik Shipstead, who took his awed constituents to lunch in the Senate dining room. Afterwards, the Mondales toured the Capitol and Fritz's dad pointed out the statue of one of his heroes, Robert M. La Follette. The future Vice President's father talked about the great crusader and reformer from Wisconsin who championed the needs of ordinary people and told his family, "There's a great man." He also took his family to Ford's Theater, where they saw

**Vice President
Walter F. Mondale
at Jimmy Carter's
home shortly after
the 1976 convention.**

Lincoln's Bible and the pistol used by his assassin. "Never forget that the gun represents the forces of evil and the Bible is always a source of constant strength to men," the father told his sons. Fritz and his brothers were properly impressed.

Walter Frederick Mondale, still nicknamed Fritz and now the Vice President of the United States, has a broad full face, little dark puffs under his eyes, a bump on his nose and a generally comfortable, rumpled look. He is sitting in a wing chair by the fireplace in his living room in Washington, wearing an old blue cardigan, casual trousers and stained suede shoes. His hair is straight, light brown with a few gray streaks and neatly trimmed.

Yes, he says, he was genuinely surprised that Jimmy Carter wanted him as his running mate. "The competition was rough, you know. Good competitors—and I didn't know Carter at all. Only met him twice, and I'd read his autobiography . . . Seemed like a good time to read it," he said, smiling at his self-effacing humor.

Walter and Joan Mondale, partners in both their private and public lives, went to Georgia the week before the Democratic national convention so Mondale could interview for the job of Carter's running mate. They spent half a day with the Carters at their home, more than an hour of which was spent by the men in private conversation in the library.

After the Mondales met the rest of the Carter family—Miss Lillian immediately expressed her approval as did brother Billy—they ate a lunch prepared by neighbor women, went on a quick tour of Plains with Jimmy at the wheel, and left town to make room for Senator John Glenn of Ohio and his wife, who were coming in for dinner with the Carters. But it was clear to the Mondales that the visit had gone well, very well. Joan Mondale hadn't even planned to go to New York for the convention, but after the visit to Plains she decided she had better go. She remembers the exact hour of the telephone call that changed the Mondales' lives.

"We were up at dawn, had breakfast, got dressed and sat there staring at the clock and waiting for the phone to ring," Mrs. Mondale says while recalling the events of Thursday, July 15. "On the dot of 8:30, the phone rang. We knew there hadn't been time for Carter to call anyone else. We knew Fritz had it."

This time, Mondale wanted the Vice Presidential nomination. In 1972, when Senator George McGovern asked him to be his running mate, Mondale declined. "I love George," Mondale explains, "but I had told him that I didn't want to be asked. I was up for re-election and had made a commitment to the people of Minnesota to run for another term."

Mondale made a wise choice. While McGovern was wiped out in the Nixon landslide, Mondale won a second term in the Senate by such a big margin that he almost brought McGovern in on his shirt tails. By now, winning was becoming a habit for Mondale. In 1960, when he was thirty-two years old and only four years out of the University of Minnesota law school, Governor Orville Freeman appointed him Attorney General despite Mondale's protests that he was too young for the job. But Free-

The Vice President was named after his great-grandfather, Frederick Mundal, who rowed his family across a Norwegian fjord to a ship bound for the United States. This photo, and the other family pictures reproduced here, are from the Mondales' personal album.

man picked him anyway, and that fall Mondale won the job on his own.

Mondale proved to be extremely popular in his new job, earning national recognition for his prosecution of charity- and price-fixing frauds and his espousal of civil rights. He won another term as Attorney General in 1962. By 1964, when his friend and political mentor, Senator Hubert Humphrey, left the Senate to become Lyndon Johnson's running mate, Mondale was the logical choice to finish Humphrey's term. Appointed by Governor Karl Rolvaag to the seat, he was elected to his first full term by a large margin in 1966.

His relatively easy wins coupled with the fact that he was appointed to both the political offices he held before becoming Vice President prompted some of Mondale's critics to suggest he leads a charmed life politically, and that his steady climb to national prominence has come without much effort on his part. Naturally, Mondale disagrees with this judgment, as does his politically astute wife.

"Fritz works hard," Joan Mondale says, with a touch of irritation in her quiet, cultured voice. "He works very hard. He always has. He does his job. He doesn't just sit around and say, oh, now it's time for me to go campaigning. He's always campaigning."

Like most people who appear to be lucky, Mondale feels that he has made much of his own luck. "You know what makes the difference?" he asks. "If you really do your job, and you work hard at it, and get yourself in a position where you can take care of a tough opponent because you've done your work, then it looks easy. If you don't do your work, if you lose touch with your constituents, and the only time they see you is when you need them, then it looks tough. And it is tough. You've let the thing deteriorate. I've always worked very, very hard to keep that relationship solid."

As a matter of fact, when his 1972 Senate victory touched off some "Mondale for President" talk, he had a big sign posted in his Senate office as a reminder to his staff: "Think Minnesota." That was at the time when Mondale first emerged as a bona fide Presidential possibility. His victory party in the Leamington Hotel ballroom in Minneapolis was dominated by Hubert Humphrey, waving his arms in the air and proclaiming, "I don't mind being John the Baptist for Walter Mondale." For a while Mondale seemed a reluctant Messiah, but as the invitations to speak came pouring in from around the country, his interest mounted, and by 1974 he began seriously testing the Presidential waters.

He soon discovered he didn't like them. He missed his family—his older son Teddy was a vulnerable sixteen then, and he felt the need to spend more time with him, his two other children and Joan. He also missed the Senate, and agonized over being absent for several key votes because of campaign trips. Mondale also didn't like being told how to speak and how to dress; a voice coach even traveled with him for a while. In September, 1974, his chances appeared to brighten considerably when Senator Edward Kennedy declared himself a non-candidate; but two months later, after returning from a trip to the Soviet Union and mulling things over at a northern Minnesota lake, Mondale decided to quit the

Fritz was about nine when he posed for this picture with his father, Theodore S. Mondale. The elder Mondale was a Methodist country minister who left his children a legacy of honesty and concern.

The young Fritz was average in the classroom but a star in basketball, football, and track. The grown-up Fritz, opposite, still loves tennis and skiing.

race. He explained that he just didn't have the "overwhelming desire to be President which is essential for the kind of campaign that is required."

When Walter Mondale came to the Senate in 1965, he was part of a new generation of young, talented and ambitious Democrats, many of whom looked on the Senate as a launching pad for even higher office— Robert and Edward Kennedy, Birch Bayh, Daniel Inouye, Gaylord Nelson, Alan Cranston, George McGovern, Ernest Hollings, Thomas Eagleton, Abraham Ribicoff. Yet, for a variety of reasons, Mondale was able to emerge from the pack. One of the reasons was undoubtedly luck, both his good luck and others' bad luck. Another was timing. But the principal reason Mondale got where he is was the impressive record of accomplishment he compiled as a legislator. The *New York Times* recently acknowledged his ability as a legislative craftsman when it declared, "Mondale is generally considered to be one of the brightest minds in the Senate . . . he does his homework."

By almost anyone's standard of measurement, Mondale had established himself as one of the most respected spokesmen for social reform and justice in America by the time he came to Jimmy Carter's attention. Starting with his maiden speech in the Senate, which addressed the world hunger problem, Mondale took up the cause of the underdog and identified himself with the politics of human needs. Time and again he prodded the public conscience about the problems of "the poor, the powerless, and those who are without adequate representation in our political system."

Mondale described himself as a "problem-oriented, pragmatic, progressive Democrat," and he constructed a career out of the issues that were the touchstones of the Democratic party's New Deal heritage—providing food, jobs, housing, education and health care for the poor and elderly; urging fair treatment for consumers and taxpayers; speaking out for the rights of children and the integrity of the family; working to preserve the environment; scrutinizing the military-industrial complex, and opposing all kinds of repression and intolerance. Such a Senator wasn't a radical but a reformer, he told the voters of Minnesota in 1972. "I haven't rejected the system," he explained. "I just want to see it work."

Nobody has worked harder during the past twelve years to make that system work than Mondale. As a legislator who understands that it is better to compromise and win half a loaf than refuse to compromise and win nothing at all, Mondale has compiled a long list of achievements that any Senator would be proud to claim.

Early in his career, he distinguished himself as a champion of consumers through his successful efforts to secure passage of the Wholesome Meat and Fair Warning Acts. His legislative skill in piloting through the Senate a controversial fair housing law won national acclaim. Mondale's early career was heavily influenced by his service with the late Robert Kennedy on Senate committees investigating hunger and malnutrition and the special educational problems of native Americans. He showed consistent concern for the rights of minorities and the disadvantaged through his work as chairman of the Senate Select Committee on Equal Educational Opportunity and the Migratory Labor Subcommittee of the Labor and Public Welfare Committee.

In recent years, as a member of the Senate Finance Committee, Mondale has fought for tax reform provisions designed to bring relief to working families, farmers and small businesses. He has been active on behalf of legislation to promote increased world trade and to promote reform of unfair trade practices affecting American businesses and workers.

Demonstrating a strong and direct interest in providing quality educational opportunities for young Americans, the former Senator has worked for liberalization of student assistance programs to cover middle income families, for adequate funding of Head Start, bilingual and other educational programs, and for greater attention to the problems of discrimination against women in the nation's educational system.

Mondale's chairmanship of the Domestic Task Force of the Senate Select Committee on Intelligence Abuses during the 94th Congress resulted in recommendations for major reforms in the activities of domestic intelligence agencies to protect the Constitutional rights and privacy of American citizens.

As chairman of the Senate Subcommittee on Children and Youth, Mondale led investigations, chaired hearings and developed legislation designed to strengthen and support American families. He was the chief Senate sponsor of the Child and Family Service Act, which would make it possible for working and poor families who want and need it to receive care for their children. Mondale was also the chief sponsor the Child

Abuse Prevention and Treatment Act and the Sudden Infant Death Syndrome Act, both enacted in 1974. Under his leadership, the subcommittee also conducted a major investigation of children's charities and a two-year examination of the state of adoption and foster care in the United States.

Mondale has also earned good marks for his work on behalf of conservation and environmental protection. Although he lost a 1973 fight for consideration of alternatives to the Trans-Alaska Oil Pipeline, subsequent findings of serious environmental and transportation difficulties in shipping crude oil from Alaska's west coast to the interior of the continental United States have justified many of the arguments he originally raised. Most of Mondale's environmental initiatives have centered on his home state of Minnesota, where he sponsored legislation that resulted in the creation of Voyagers National Park, the St. Croix Wild and Scenic Riverway and, most recently, the Minnesota Valley Wildlife Refuge and Recreation Area. Of national significance is a Mondale-authored program for protection and restoration of the nation's fresh-water lakes created under the 1972 Federal Water Pollution Control Act Amendments, and the Wild and Scenic River Study of the Upper Mississippi.

One of the most controversial aspects of Mondale's Senate career has been his stand on school desegregation. In 1970, when the school busing issue was at a heated pitch, Mondale took to the Senate floor to urge his colleagues not to stand "in the schoolhouse door" to bar black children. "Busing is the means—at times the only means—by which segregation in public education can be reduced," he declared in a speech that his critics seized on to justify calling him "Mr. Busing."

Mondale didn't expect his stand on busing to be popular, but he finds it perplexing that some people still consider him an advocate of forced busing as a means of achieving racial equality in public schools. "I've never been hot for busing, but there was a real panic setting in," Mondale explains. "Congress was getting ready to pass legislation which I thought was not only fruitless but destructive, with respect to prohibiting discrimination in schools. So I just went over and gave about a ten-minute speech. I just didn't see how we could justify ripping a page out of the Constitution and saying, in effect, this time you *can* discriminate. My point is, we ought to trust the courts, let the courts handle law, and the speech I gave laid out that theory."

Mondale is proud of his record in civil rights, particularly his work as chairman of the Equal Educational Opportunity Committee, whose two years of hearings and final report were an important factor in the drive to complete the task of desegregating the nation's schools.

At the same time, he has learned from painful experience that it is just as easy to move too slowly in taking a stand on an issue as it is to move too quickly. "The biggest mistake I've made since I began my public life was not seeing the folly of the Vietnam war more quickly than I did," he says. Although he finally took a strong stand against the war in 1969, he concedes that "if only more of us had perceived the

Surrounded by a small forest of undecorated Christmas trees, Walter Mondale married Joan Adams on December 27, 1955, fifty-three days after they met.

tragedy of Vietnam earlier, maybe we could have brought the war to an end sooner than we did. I've never forgotten that mistake."

Perhaps that mistake made Mondale quicker to perceive the abuses of Watergate and to recognize the threat to the Constitution that it presented. He took a leading role in campaign reform and in pushing for public financing of political campaigns. "As devastating as Watergate was," Mondale says, "it also gave me a new sense of optimism about this country. The Constitutional processes worked and the system was able to overthrow the yoke of a President who thought he was above the law." The Watergate experience led Mondale to write a book—his first—in which he advocates a better balancing of Presidential power with legislative and judicial power and more stringent safeguards on the executive branch, as well as substantial changes in the primary and general election laws.

The book, titled *The Accountability of Power—Toward a Responsible Presidency,* was published in early 1976. Those who have watched Mondale over the years feel it reflects the thinking of a mature and realistic legislator who understands that despite all the good intentions in the world, many problems facing government today are so difficult and complex that politicians should not promise solutions, but only promise to seek solutions.

Mondale does not discourge such an interpretation. "We don't have the ambitious rhetoric of the early 1960's anymore," he says. "We're still committed, but we have more modest expectations than in those early, heady days. I was part of those days, starting as a young Attorney General, so I look back on them with a great deal of fondness. But today the issues are so incredibly involved. How do you solve the energy crisis? How do you get full employment and yet abate inflation? How do you make government work more efficiently? How do you educate a poor kid? All those questions that seemed so easy before we tried have proven to be much more difficult once we've tried."

These are deep and disturbing questions, and neither Mondale nor those around him pretend to know the answers. "Some people expect him to work miracles," one aide says in a reference to those liberal Democrats who look to the new Democratic administration to solve the nation's most pressing social and economic problems. "But he's never been able to work miracles and he's not going to now."

When Walter Mondale was asked at the press conference that introduced him as Jimmy Carter's running mate if he thought he would make a good President, he replied, "I hope and pray I would be." But he added, "I don't know."

Mondale's unflinching honesty about his own talents and abilities and his realistic assessment of the nature of the Vice Presidency make it unlikely that he will be surprised if the office turns out to be different than advertised. He feels he has a genuinely close personal relationship with Jimmy Carter and is confident that Carter will continue to give him a major role in his administration. But he is also aware of the

The Mondale's first child was Teddy, above, who is now 19. William, 14, was six when photographed below with his dad.

inherent difficulties of a job that has inspired a huge storehouse of comic stories and derogatory folklore. "The whole story of the Vice Presidency can be summed up in the fact that Presidents usually don't share power very easily, or very gracefully," says a veteran watcher of Presidents and Vice Presidents. "The whole story of the Mondale Vice Presidency is, will it be any different this time?"

There is ample evidence that it will. Politics more than anything else is about character and personality, both of which were important factors in the selection of Walter Mondale. Mondale knows perhaps as well as anyone who has ever been there the promises and pitfalls of the office, having benefited from a close observation of Hubert Humphrey's painfully-acquired experience in the job and of each succeeding Vice President. He is also confident that his relationship with Carter not only allows, but requires, honest expression of his viewpoints if he is to fulfill his role as the President's top adviser. "If I'm not totally honest and willing to be the bearer of bad news when it is necessary, what good am I to him?" Mondale asks.

Fritz and Joan beam as they learn of Mondale's appointment to the Senate seat vacated by his political mentor, Hubert Humphrey, when Humphrey became Vice President in 1964.

Mondale's scratchy honesty and flinty integrity come from his father, Theodore Sigvaard Mondale, who taught his sons one uncompromising lesson: "You can make mistakes around here, but you can't lie."

"Around here" was the farmland of southern Minnesota, at the Iowa border, the corn-and-soybean country that the Reverend Mr. Mondale traveled as a rural Methodist minister. His mission took him and his family through a series of small towns, little patches on the vast landscape, the crunch of midwestern plainness mixed with northern poetry in the names: Ceylon, Heron Lake, Elmore. The Mondales came from the great Scandinavian migration to this country in the last century, when nearly half the population of Norway set out for the new land, sending a higher proportion of its people here than any other country except Ireland. A color photograph of the Mondale land in Norway—there, the unanglicized name was Mundal—has hung in his Senate office, the waters of Sogne Fjord icy blue, the mountain slicing right down to the water. "My great-grandfather Frederick and his family, including three kids, got in a rowboat, rowed several hours to where they got a ship, and came to the United States," Mondale remembers. "And there was never a Mondale back in that valley for over a hundred years." When one went back, it was the Senator, taking his wife along on the voyage into his own rich past. He will take the picture with him to his White House office.

When Frederick and his family landed, they kept going west to Wisconsin, La Follette country, where many Scandinavians settled. One of Frederick's boys, Ole, grew up and married a Norwegian girl, and they filed a claim for a piece of land near Blue Earth, where they raised a large family, including the Vice President's father, Theodore. Theodore married twice. The three sons and an adopted daughter of his first marriage were nearly grown when his wife died and he married Claribel Cowan, a music teacher whom he'd met at church. They had three sons. Their middle child, born on January 5, 1928, in an old two-story frame house in the tiny town of Ceylon, Minnesota, was named Walter Frederick and nicknamed Fritz, after his pioneer ancestor who had left the Mundal valley in a crowded rowboat.

But the family legacy involves more than a name. Besides that unswerving honesty, there is a personal reticence, a sense of self-effacement so deep as to be sometimes detrimental. "One of the reasons he dropped out in 1974," says a man who knows Mondale well, "is that he just didn't think he'd necessarily make a better President than anybody else."

There is a lack of interest in money. The Reverend Mr. Mondale served poor, rural parishes; his boys bartered corn and cabbages door to door in nearby Blue Earth. Their house in Elmore—where Fritz spent most of his childhood—was heated with cobs, coal being too expensive. Nobody thought about being poor; they didn't think about money at all, just built a trailer, painted it aluminum and went to Washington. Now, Vice President Mondale owns no real estate except an unpretentious stucco house in a fashionable northwest Washington neighborhood, still mortgaged. He has no business interests, direct or indirect, no stocks or bonds. His wife has worked part-time as a bus tour guide on tourist buses, not out of boredom but because, like other middle-aged, middle-class couples, they needed the money. In 1974, they took out a bank loan to tide them over.

There is in this family an attitude of conciliation, of getting along. Fritz's older brother, Clarence "Pete" Mondale, now a neighbor of Fritz's and chairman of the Department of Experimental Programs at George Washington University, once called their father "the least vindictive man I've ever known. He didn't have the least impulse for vengeance, for getting back at the other guy. It was part of his feeling of emphasizing people's strengths, not getting into unnecessary fights. He chose conciliation over confrontation both with his parishioners and in his family. It was a way of life with him."

Most of all, there is the commitment to justice that Fritz Mondale absorbed at the family supper table. The father didn't lecture; he just lived his life, as it was. "He never lived inside his own skin," Fritz's younger brother, William "Mort" Mondale, now an official of the South Dakota Education Association, has said. "He was always completely concerned with other people." But the country preacher who made sandwiches for the hobo at the back door didn't try to convert the hobo; he simply saw him, and talked of him as someone whose life was important. The talks were simple and low-keyed. "Dad wasn't prudent in the sense of saving against tomorrow," says Pete Mondale. "But he had a kind of faith in the future, a sort of expectancy that something good is going to come of all this. He used to say, 'Be a wise steward.' "

The sense of stewardship that Walter Mondale inherited from his father has deeply influenced his political philosophy and his approach to government. By the lights of the religious and ethical environment that the Mondale boys lived in, the individual was supremely important, a precious "kind of semi-divinity not to be taken lightly," according to

The Mondales' middle child is Eleanor, 16, photographed here with her father on the grounds of the Lincoln Memorial in 1974.

Pete Mondale. This belief manifested itself in a kind of excitement the Reverend Mr. Mondale felt about what a person might become if given the opportunity to develop his native abilities. It was an attitude that perhaps more than anything would account for the future Vice President's concern for the disadvantaged and save him being too vulnerable to more cynical explanations of his espousal of the underprivileged. "The kind of talk that we heard at home can be empty rhetoric or it can be serious business," says Pete Mondale. "With Dad, it was pretty serious business." Fritz's oldest half-brother Lester, one of three sons and a daughter from his father's first marriage, puts it another way: "If Fritz were anything but Mr. Clean, Dad would be turning over in his grave."

As a Senator, Mondale earned a reputation as an ardent spokesman for the poor and powerless. Here, he speaks at a 1972 Senate hearing.

Mondale's mother was a different, but equally influential, force in shaping his life. A very self-reliant, independent-minded person, she was interested in music and her family more than politics. A graduate of Northwestern University with a major in music, she conducted the church choirs, ran the Sunday School classes, watched for needy families and persons in the parish, and kept the Mondale family on an even keel. After Fritz's father died in 1948, Mrs. Mondale went to work and provided a home for her children. Fritz lived with her in St. Paul when he was attending law school and he remained close to her until her death in 1967.

Before he was Mr. Clean, he was Crazylegs. They called him that in the 1946 high school yearbook at Elmore, where the family moved when Fritz was in sixth grade.

These were good, healthy years. Fritz and his brothers tipped over outhouses on Hallowe'en and raised a normal amount of what is called in the Midwest "the dickens." At school Fritz was only average in the classroom, although a superstar in sports. Always, there was music in the house, and laughing. Fritz's tenor voice was encouraged by his mother, and when one of his best buddies, Gene Kelly, was married, Fritz sang "The Lord's Prayer" and "Bless This House" at the wedding.

Mondale was raised on reform politics; Theodore, who had been a Republican before he lost two farms in the 1920's, turned to the New Deal and even, for a while, to Norman Thomas. "The Republicans did him in," Mondale says wryly, of his father; one of Mondale's first political programs involved changing the procedures by which farm mortgages could be foreclosed.

For anybody who thrived on progressive politics, Minnesota was the place. The state has been a center of protest since Civil War days, when the Minnesota Grange was formed in an attempt to disassociate the fate of farmers from the decisions of eastern bankers and railroad men. In enlightened Minnesota, politics has always been an honorable career.

Walter Mondale was still a student at Macalester College in St. Paul when he got his first practical experience in politics by helping the Democratic-Farmer-Labor Party pack precincts and wrest control of the party from Communist sympathizers and extreme leftists. In 1948, Mondale volunteered to work for Hubert Humphrey's first Senate campaign, and was sent to organize the southern Minnesota congressional district

Mondale stumps for the Democratic ticket, above, in August, 1976. Below, he pauses to converse with another Vice President.

where Elmore was located. Humphrey won the district and was elected, along with a new DFL congressman from St. Paul named Eugene McCarthy. Later, after Mondale replaced Humphrey in the Senate and joined McCarthy there, he would be caught in the crossfire of their differing stands on the Vietnam war.

When Humphrey was elected, Fritz Mondale took a year off from Macalester, where he'd been working his way through by some usual routes—dishwashing—and some unusual—inspecting for pea lice at a cannery. He went to Washington for a year to work for Americans for Democratic Action, went back to school, then joined the Army and spent two years at Fort Knox, joining as a private and coming out a corporal. He enrolled in law school the day after getting out of the Army.

On a blind date he met Joan Adams, a classmate's sister, who lectured at the Minneapolis Institute of Fine Arts. They went to the picture exhibit "The Family of Man," assembled by Edward Steichen. Fifty-three days later they were married.

It was a Presbyterian wedding, Joan's choice. "I said, I'm the one who will raise the children," she explains now. "I said, I'm the one who will take them to Sunday school. So I want to take them to the church I feel most comfortable in. It just makes more sense in the family to do it that way."

She has taken the children all sorts of places since. She has changed diapers and storm windows and taken the car in for tune-ups. She has just painted their house, which they'll rent out while they're living in what she calls "the big deal house," the Vice President's mansion. She's done a lot, for twenty years, including watching the budget closely. Still, she says, "I've had a very satisfying adult life of my own. I've never just sat around, drinking coffee with my neighbors. I've never done that. Eleanor Jane was born in January of 1960, and that fall I went out campaigning. I left her with a babysitter. And I did it again in 1962. I was gone three days out of five. But there hasn't been any pain. No unpleasant experiences. Everything seems to work out so well."

Eleanor is sixteen now, with long blonde hair, crazy about horses. Teddy Mondale was three when his Dad was appointed Attorney General of Minnesota. Now he's nineteen, working in the fruit and vegetable section at the Giant market, not sure whether he wants to go to college, not sure what he wants to do. William is fourteen, with an active social life. The obvious irony, pointed out to Walter Mondale more often than he probably likes to hear, is that for a staunch proponent of the American family, he has spent so little time with his own.

"I know that," he says now, hearing it again. "And maybe I got involved with family issues in politics because of guilt feelings." He looks into the fire, then across the room toward his wife.

"It's a tough thing, you know, when you're in elective office," he says quietly. "You try to make time with the family, go skiing together, but it's never satisfactory. It just isn't. I remember, one day I was sitting next to Phil Hart at a hearing on the CIA, and I said, 'You know, Phil, my kid's playing football today.' And Phil said, 'You get up and leave this room right now, because when I look back on my life, that's the dumbest thing I ever did—not giving my family more of my time.'" Mondale pauses for a moment. "So I left. I just walked out of the hearing and I got to the stadium just as William intercepted a pass. The kid made twenty yards and got tackled, right at my feet. He looked up, and I was there."

"You knew what the life was like," his wife says. "We knew that." He nods a little. No illusions.

"The important thing is why you want to go into politics. If you go into it for money, or vanity, or power, it's a dreadful thing to inflict on yourself and on your family. I'm not all pure—I'm talking about tendencies. If you want to try to help, you're going to be all right.

"It's easy to lose your way in public life, you know. In public life you can get caught up in the posturing and the puffing, and your head can get turned by the flattery. Or you can get twisted and poisoned by the backbiting and the competition and the disappointments. What's important is just to remember who you are and do your best and be content with that. That's all you can do; otherwise it'll destroy you." He pauses again. "I've got some friends who have been destroyed by it.

"You know, the reputation of politicians in America absolutely couldn't be worse. Crooks, cheaters, self-servers. But I'll tell you this.

One of the most reassuring things for me has been the degree to which the people I've worked with are properly motivated, even though I may not agree with them.

"But I really believe that when the history of these last ten or fifteen years is finally written, and the next generation can pass judgment dispassionately, this grimy, sweaty snake rassle called politics— and the politicians—are going to come out of this in pretty good shape, as the people who really held the society together, kept working on the problems, trying to reform our institutions, and our programs, trying to make them work. There is a validity to the political process, and the politicians in it, that I think from a historical perspective is going to look pretty good. Not that we're perfect. But the profession is a good one, and it's the best way, though imperfect, to get to the kind of solutions that people need. I feel good about it."

Pleased and comfortable with each other, the President and Vice President were photographed at Plains, Georgia in August of 1976.

INAUGURATIONS

The weather may be changeable but the high promise of the moment is always the same

by RICHARD M. KETCHUM

It was Will Rogers who reminded us that, "Presidents become great, but they have to be made Presidents first," and the last step in that often supremely difficult process is when the newly elected Chief Executive takes the thirty-five word oath prescribed by the Constitution. It is a majestic moment, and not least because it places this individual in the select line of men who have held the destinies of the nation in their hands for nearly two centuries. In 1789, when George Washington first repeated that oath, Great Britain and France were ruled by kings, much of Europe by a Holy Roman Emperor, Russia by a tsarina, China by an emperor, Japan by a shogun. All are gone now, save for the British monarch, holding an office changed almost beyond recognition, whereas the office assumed by President Carter is essentially the same as the one assumed by by President Washington.

Presidents have taken the oath in a variety of different places, including the portico of the Capitol, the "back porch" of the White House, a farmhouse in Vermont, a brownstone in New York City, on board a jet airplane, and in all kinds of weather and circumstances. But wherever and however that solemn event occurs, it has elements of elation and of high promise on the one hand; sadness and sometimes tragedy on the other. The oath-taking, of course, punctuates a moment that is like the passing of monarchs: the king is dead, long live the king. Indeed, the inauguration ceremonies, as they have evolved over the years, have been called by an English historian America's quadrennial coronation.

The inauguration is something of a catharsis for the American people—an act of healing after the divisiveness of a political campaign. Through all the pageantry and whoop-de-do comes the message that although one side has lost, the leader of the other side is going to do everything possible to unite the nation behind him. The inauguration is the most visible affirmation we have of our faith in institutions, and when it is over, one more symbolic act is taken. The new President's home that night is the nation's home—the most historic building in Washington, D.C.—and he sleeps where every President since John Adams has rested. Because he is there, that house is a symbol of power and sovereignty, but it is also the home of a man and his family—the one man who represents us all.

Cheers echoed through New York, church bells pealed and cannon boomed when Washington took his first oath of office at Federal Hall. Amos Doolittle made this engraving—the only contemporary rendition of the event—from a sketch by an eyewitness.

Rowed across New York harbor for his inauguration, the first President received a tumultuous greeting.

1789 On February 4, the electors in each state of the new United States met to cast their ballots, and all sixty-nine of them voted for George Washington for President. (John Adams of Massachusetts, who received thirty-four votes, was to be Vice President.) Congress settled upon March 4 as the date for the new government to come into existence, at which time, it was proposed, Congress would convene in New York and the president pro tem of the Senate would officially open the ballots and declare George Washington the unanimous choice. Unfortunately, March 4 came and went and it was some weeks later before a quorum was present. ("The delay is inauspicious to say the best of it," was Washington's opinion.) Finally, on April 4, Irishman Charles Thomson, the secretary of the Congress, rode up to Mount Vernon, greeted Washington, made a solemn little speech informing him that he had been chosen to lead the nation, and handed him formal notification in the form of a letter from John Langdon, president pro tem of the Senate.

After agreeing to accept the electors' offer, the land-poor Washington borrowed five hundred pounds to pay off his debts, borrowed another hundred pounds for the expenses of the trip to New York, and two days later climbed into his coach and departed from his beloved Mount Vernon. He felt, he said, not unlike "a culprit who is going to the place of his execution."

On April 30, 1789, almost two months behind schedule, Congress finally completed arrangements for the inauguration of the nation's first President. George Washington, after having his hair powdered, dressed carefully in a suit of brown cloth woven for him in Connecticut, white silk stockings, and silverbuckled shoes, fastened a dress sword at his side, put his inaugural address in an inner pocket, entered the huge state coach provided by Congress, and was driven to Federal Hall, where the Senators and Representatives waited. In the Senate chamber, John Adams escorted him to a chair on the dais and, after formally welcoming Washington and announcing that the oath of office would be administered by Robert R. Livingston, Chancellor of the State of

New York, the Vice President led the way to a porticoed balcony overlooking Wall Street. As far as the eye could see, people filled the streets, and Washington, placing his hand on the Bible, repeated after Livingston the thirty-five words required by the Constitution:

"I do solemnly swear that I will faithfully execute the Office of President of the United States, and will to the best of my Ability, preserve, protect and defend the Constitution of the United States."

"I swear, so help me God," he added in a grave voice, and as he bowed to kiss the Bible Livingston proclaimed, "It is done." Then, with a broad gesture to the crowd, he shouted loud and clear, "Long live George Washington, President of the United States!"

John Adams

1797 If ever a man worried about appearances it was John Adams, and on the occasion of his inauguration he had every cause to do so. So short and chubby he was known as "His Rotundity," he stood nervously alongside three six-footers—his predecessor George Washington, Thomas Jefferson, Vice President by dint of a narrow loss to Adams, and Chief Justice Oliver Ellsworth, who was to administer the oath of office. Not only that; when Adams arrived for the ceremony, dressed to the nines, he found many members of Congress in tears. They had eyes not for the new President but for the old—the man who had come alone to Congress Hall in a plain black coat and was seated by himself on the platform when Adams entered. Ever alert for a slight, Adams wrote his wife that Washington seemed "to enjoy a triumph over me. Methought I heard

him say, 'Ay! I'm fairly out and you fairly in. See which of us will be happiest!'"

After the President-elect was escorted to his temporary residence by Jefferson, Washington made his way through the crowd to congratulate Adams. The throng watched him enter the building and as he disappeared inside a great roar went up—a noise, one man wrote, like "a sound of thunder." And that evening the merchants of Philadelphia gave a banquet not for Adams, but for Washington. Even so, when it was all over, Adams—to his credit—could write that "what they call the Inauguration" had been "the sublimest Thing ever exhibited in America."

1809 "Jemmy Madison—ah! poor Jemmy!" wrote Washington Irving. "He is but a withered little apple-John." James Madison may have been known as the Father of the Constitution, and he may have been the only Chief Executive to face enemy gunfire while in office, but at 5'4" and weighing less than 100 pounds he was not an imposing figure. He was, in fact, the smallest President in U.S. history and at his inauguration, it was said, Chief Justice John Marshall stared at him so scornfully that Madison blushed. Whether Marshall was disgusted because of Madison's size or because he was a Democrat-Republican is not recorded. The great jurist, a staunch Federalist, administered the oath nine times to five Presidents—Jefferson, Madison, Monroe, and Jackson twice each, and John Quincy Adams once.

1829 In the long history of Presidential inaugurations, nothing has equalled Andrew Jackson's. From all over the country the common folk poured into the capital to see their hero, Old Hickory, sworn in. "I have never seen such a crowd before," Daniel Webster wrote. "Persons have come five hundred miles to see General Jackson, and they really seem to think that the country has been rescued from some dreadful danger." Jackson's beloved wife, Rachel, had died recently, so no inaugural ball was planned; instead, the President-elect decided to hold open house at the Executive Mansion for his partisans.

And by the hundreds they came, "immense crowds of all sorts of people, from the highest and the most polished, down to the most vulgar and gross in the nation," wrote Supreme Court Justice Joseph Story. "I never saw such a mixture. The reign of KING MOB seemed triumphant." Into the President's House the horde streamed, and as one observer reported, "Orange punch by barrels full was made, but as the waiters opened the door to bring it out, a rush would be made, the glasses broken, the pails of liquor upset, and the most painful confusion prevailed. . . . On such an occasion it was certainly difficult to keep anything like order, but it was mortifying to see men, with boots heavy with mud, standing on the damask satin covered chairs, from their eagerness to get a sight of the President." There was such a press to shake Jackson's hand that he was trapped, almost suffocating, unable to free himself. A group of men finally formed a cordon around him and, locking arms, drove a wedge through the crowd and out a back door, returning the President exhausted but safe to his rooms at Gadsby's Tavern. Meanwhile, servants carried food out onto the lawn to draw the mob out of the White House.

1841 The log cabin and hard cider were the symbols of his campaign, even though he lived in a twenty-two-room clapboarded house and drank no cider. At sixty-eight William Henry Harrison was the oldest man to be elected President, but the honor brought no joy to his wife. "I wish my husband's friends had left him happy and contented where he was," she said.

March 4, 1841, was bitterly cold, but the hero of Tippecanoe refused to ride to the Capitol in a carriage. Mounted on what John Quincy Adams called "a mean-looking white horse," he rode "in the centre of seven others, in a plain frock-coat or surtout, undistinguishable from any of those before, behind or around him." He wore no hat and delivered the longest inaugural address in history; written for him by Daniel Webster, it lasted two hours. The exposure and the exertion of preparing for office proved too much. One month later he was dead—the first President to die in office.

President Harrison (a tiny figure on the reviewing stand) spoke for two hours at his inauguration. He died exactly one month later.

A full-rigged miniature of the USS Constitution was part of James Buchanan's inaugural parade.

1857 According to most authorities, the inauguration of James Buchanan was an absolutely brilliant affair. A crowd of 150,000 was on hand—including representatives from New Mexico, Utah, Washington, and Oregon territories. It was a bright, beautiful day; the scarlet-coated Marine Band and a battalion of Marines led off the parade, followed by a rather wondrous float—a full-rigged miniature of the frigate *Constitution*. Spectators tossed flowers into the open barouche carrying the two handsome Presidents—Franklin Pierce and the six-foot, white-haired Buchanan. During the afternoon there was a balloon ascension by an astronaut named Mr. Eliot, and that evening the bachelor President and his niece, Harriet Lane, presided over what has been called the first truly successful inaugural ball. The specially built structure, 235 feet long and 77 feet wide, in which it was held was lined with red, white, and blue draperies and the flags of many nations. A ceiling of white cloth, punctured with golden stars, was lit with the warm glow of enormous gaslight chandeliers. In the center of the room reposed a cake four feet high decorated with the flags of each American state and territory, and the guests were offered huge quantities of wine and everything else, including 400 gallons of oysters and 1,200 quarts of ice cream. Dancing went on until dawn and when the Democrats finally left, they carried off warm memories of a splendid occasion. It was just as well. The next inauguration of a Democratic President was to be twenty-eight years later.

Beneath the surface of Buchanan's glittering celebration, things were quite different. Naval surgeon Jonathan Foltz was never far from the President-elect's side during the day or evening; he was treating his patient for the same gastro-intestinal ailment that had struck a number of political figures. Known as the "National Hotel disease," it was believed to have been caused by rats contaminating the water supply of that building. But dysentery was the least of the capital's problems. The nation was divided as never before, and the Russian minister, dancing with the French ambassador's wife, sensed it. "We are dancing on a volcano," he told her.

1861 A group of New York merchants had presented a fourteen-foot open barouche to Abraham Lincoln and in it he rode, with retiring President James Buchanan, to his inauguration, despite the hazards of doing so. Seven Southern states had already seceded; the President-elect had had to enter Washington by an unannounced route because of a suspected plot to kill him; the commanding general of the army had insisted on unprecedented security precautions for the inauguration, so that Pennsylvania Avenue bristled with soldiers and guns.

While Lincoln, beneath the unfinished Capitol dome, read the address in which he assured the South that the government "will not assail you," his old debating foe Stephen A. Douglas held his top hat. In the crowd listening to the speech were four men who would one day take the same oath of office—Rutherford B. Hayes, James A. Garfield, Chester A. Arthur, and Benjamin Harrison.

Four years later, the weather was so bad that Pennsylvania Avenue was a bottomless sea of mud. The Army Corps of Engineers even considered laying pontoons to form a bridge between the White House and the Capitol, and pedestrians who could not swim were warned to stay on the sidewalks. Even so, more than thirty thousand people stood in the mire to hear Lincoln deliver what was probably the noblest speech in history by a victorious leader. Six weeks later, on April 14, 1865, the Lincolns rode to Ford's Theater in the same carriage used at his first inauguration.

Beneath the uncompleted Capitol dome, Lincoln gave his first inaugural speech to an uneasy Washington on the eve of war.

1877 In the election of 1876, Rutherford B. Hayes's popular vote was 250,000 less than that of his Democratic opponent, Samuel Tilden, but the electoral votes of several Southern states and Oregon were challenged and a special Electoral Commission was appointed to determine whether the disputed votes belonged to Hayes or Tilden. At four A.M. on March 2, 1877, in the House of Representatives, Hayes was declared the winner by one vote—185 to 184. Immediately, Tilden's supporters urged their man to assume the office forcibly, if necessary, and there were rumors that he would take the oath as President on Sunday, March 4.

On Saturday afternoon, Hayes and his daughter attended a matinee performance of *Il Trovatore* in Washington, and that evening he and Mrs. Hayes arrived at the White House to dine with the Grants and some thirty other guests. After dinner, while Mrs. Grant entertained the others, President Grant, President-elect Hayes, and Chief Justice Morrison B. Waite disappeared into the Red Room, where Hayes quietly took the oath of office. It was the only time in history that the nation technically had two Presidents, and the first time a President-elect was sworn in before the designated date. On Monday, March 5, the Chief Justice officially administered the oath of office to President Hayes on the east steps of the Capitol building, and to everyone's great relief, no disturbances marred the occasion.

**Rutherford B. Hayes
and his teetotaling wife, Lucy.**

Hayes's wife, Lucy, was known as "Lemonade Lucy" because of her ban on alcoholic beverages in the White House; she and her deeply religious husband held prayer readings every morning after breakfast and their favorite diversion was hymn singing on Sunday nights—occasions attended by cabinet members and Congressmen. The first telephone was installed in the White House during Hayes's term and Lucy began the tradition of egg-rolling on the White House lawn. But Hayes was not sorry to depart after one term. "Nobody ever left the Presidency," he observed, "with less regret, less disappointment, [and] fewer heartburnings . . . than I do."

1881 At the urging of his mother, who had raised him in a log cabin, James A. Garfield worked as a janitor at Western Reserve Eclectic Institute in Ohio, went on to Williams College, and on the way to becoming a scholar acquired the knack of writing Latin with one hand while simultaneously writing Greek with the other. His mother was the first to see her son inaugurated as President of the United States, and immediately after taking the oath Garfield kissed his parent, kissed his wife, Lucretia, and with the two women at his side, reviewed the grand procession from what was surely one of the most ornate stands ever erected for the occasion.

Like his predecessor, Garfield discovered that he had no fondness for the Presidency: "My God!" he exclaimed. "What is there in this place that a man should ever want to get into it?" He seems to have had a premonition of his own death; two days before he was assassinated he summoned Robert Todd Lincoln, the late President's son, and asked him to relate his memories of the shooting of his father. When Garfield himself was shot in September, 1881, his mother asked, "How could anybody be so cold-hearted as to want to kill my baby?"

1885 Grover Cleveland's record was studded with "firsts": the first President to serve for two terms that were not consecutive; the first to ride to and from the Capitol in two inaugurations accompanied both times by the same President (Harrison, who succeeded Cleveland in 1889, traveled the route with him that year and again four years later, when Cleveland succeeded him). Cleveland was the first Democratic Presi-

One of history's most ornate Presidential reviewing stands was that of James Garfield,
who watched his inaugural parade with his wife and mother by his side.

dent since Buchanan. Like Buchanan, he was a bachelor, and he was the first President to be married in the White House. And as one wag remarked, he was the first President who was able to remove his shirt without unbuttoning his collar (at 5'11" and just under 300 pounds, Cleveland had a corpulent figure and a huge bull neck).

When Cleveland succeeded Chester Arthur in 1885 they were driven to the Capitol in an open barouche behind Arthur's magnificent matched bays by Albert Hawkins, who was the White House coachman under Grant, Hayes, Garfield, Arthur and Cleveland. One of the first things Cleveland did when he moved into the White House was to measure the hay in the stables and send Arthur a check for it. The following year he married Frances Folsom, the daughter of his late law partner; he was forty-nine years old and she was not yet twenty-two, and he waited until she graduated from college before asking for her

hand. When they vacated the White House in 1889 to make way for the Benjamin Harrisons, Frances Cleveland told a steward, "I want you to take good care of all the furniture and ornaments in the house, for I want to find everything just as it is now when we come back again. For we are coming back just four years from today." And so they did, just as she had said.

1897 It is probable that the inauguration of William McKinley was the only such occasion when the outgoing President wore only one shoe. Grover Cleveland was suffering from gout and had to lean heavily on his successor's arm as they entered the Senate chamber.

McKinley was another of those hapless Presidents who found, at their inauguration, that most of the cheers were for another man—in McKinley's case, for Teddy Roosevelt, the Rough Rider and popular hero. He also discovered, as so many others before and after him did, that the opinion he had formed of the Presidency before taking office was quite unlike the reality. On his first inauguration day he turned to Cleveland and said, enthusiastically, "What an impressive thing it is to assume tremendous responsibilities!" Two years later, he complained, "I have had enough of it, Heaven knows! I have had all the honor there is in this place, and have had responsibilities enough to kill a man."

1913 Perhaps no outgoing President left office with more relief than William Howard Taft, who had always really wanted to be Chief Justice of the United States—an appointment that came to him in 1921. On the way to the Capitol with President-elect Woodrow Wilson, he smiled broadly and chatted with his successor, giving him a number of tips about the Presidency, including the information that the financial burdens of the office were light. For the Tafts—Helen Taft, especially—the White House years had been a bitter disappointment. She suffered a severe stroke in 1909 and the President, during her slow recovery, had lovingly taught her to speak again. He and his once-close friend Teddy Roosevelt had become enemies, and Roosevelt bolted the Republican Party to run on the Progressive "Bull Moose" ticket to deny Taft reelection.

For the Wilsons, the first night in the White House was a joyous one, and there was "a continuous running through the house, from one room to another, a shrill voice screaming to someone else as a new place was discovered" by one or another of the three daughters—all single and in their twenties.

1923 Calvin Coolidge's swearing in as President had every hallmark of the all-American Horatio Alger story—the old family farmhouse in the hamlet of Plymouth Notch in Vermont's Green Mountains, the family Bible, the parlor lighted by a kerosene lamp, and his father, a notary public and farmer, administering the oath. In the early hours of August 3, 1923, 78-year-old John Coolidge was awakened by a knock on the kitchen door. He called to his son, who went downstairs, opened the door to find a Western Union agent from eight miles away, and read the telegram that told him of Harding's death. Before long some newspaper reporters

showed up; the local telephone operator was asked to put through a call to Washington to the Attorney General, who dictated the exact words of the oath of office, and at 2:47 A.M. John Coolidge swore in his son Calvin as the thirtieth President of the United States.

About fifteen minutes later, two men from the telephone company arrived and installed a telephone for the President, who used it to call the Secretary of State. By 7 A.M. Calvin and Grace Coolidge were dressed and eating breakfast, and soon were on their way to catch a train to Washington. When they were gone, John Coolidge picked up the new telephone and told the operator he wanted it removed right away. And so began an administration characterized by Coolidge's belief that "if you don't say anything, you won't be called on to repeat it."

1933 During Grover Cleveland's first term, one of his New York constituents paid a call on him, accompanied by his five-year-old son. "My little man," the President told the youngster, "I am making a strange wish for you. I hope that you may never be President of the United States." Apparently Cleveland did not wish hard enough, for the boy went on to become President not once, but four times—more than any other man in the history of the nation.

At his first inauguration, on March 4, 1933, the nation was—in contrast to its buoyant mood four years earlier—near panic, gripped by the worst economic depression it had ever experienced. In his address Franklin D. Roosevelt re-

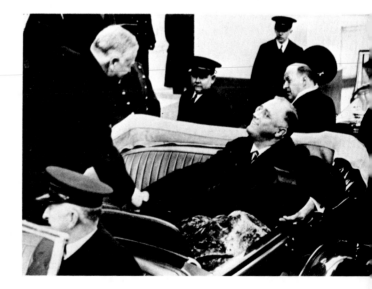

assured Americans that "this great nation will endure as it has endured, will revive and will prosper. So, first of all, let me assert my firm belief that the only thing we have to fear is fear itself..." As Will Rogers observed, "America hasn't been as happy in three years as they are today. No money, no banks, no worry, no nothing, but they know they got a man in there who is wise to Congress and wise to our so-called big men. The whole country is with him. Even if what he does is wrong they are with him. Just so he does something. If he burned down the capitol we would cheer and say, 'Well, we at least got a fire started, anyhow'."

On the day before the inauguration there had been a tense encounter between incoming and outgoing Presidents. Traditionally, the incumbent Chief Executive invited his successor to dine at the White House, but Hoover, bitter about his election loss, refused to extend an invitation. Finally, he was persuaded by the White House usher, Irwin Hoover, that he should give Roosevelt the opportunity to pay his respects, and at the last minute FDR received an invitation to tea. He and Eleanor, his wife, and their eldest son, James, arrived, and after spending an uncomfortable hour with the Hoovers, Roosevelt tried to make a graceful gesture as he prepared to leave. Crippled by polio and unable to walk without assistance, he said, "Mr. President, as you know it is rather difficult for me to move in a hurry. It takes me a little while to get up and I know how busy you must be, sir, so please don't wait for me."

Hoover, unable or unwilling to concede anything to his rival, said bleakly, "Mr. Roosevelt,

after you have been President for a while, you will learn that the President of the United States waits for no one." And with that he strode from the room. The next morning, when the two Presidents rode from the White House to the Capitol, the atmosphere between them was as chilly as the day. That was the last time a Presidential inauguration took place in March; beginning with FDR's second inauguration, all have been held on January 20.

1961 John F. Kennedy was the first Catholic and, at forty-three, the youngest man to be elected President (Theodore Roosevelt was forty-two when he succeeded McKinley at the time of the latter's death, but he was not elected until he was forty-six). A storm had deposited six inches of snow on the capital the day before Kennedy's inauguration, and three thousand servicemen worked through the night to clear the Pennsylvania Avenue parade route. Along with the scheduled events, two entirely unexpected incidents made the inaugural scene a memorable one for the crowds at the ceremony and for millions of Americans watching on television: Robert Frost, blinded by the bright sun on the snow, unable to read the poem he had composed for the occasion, reciting another from memory; and smoke rising from the lectern while Richard Cardinal Cushing delivered the invocation. While the prelate prayed on, Secret Service men and firemen crawled around the platform and finally succeeded in locating the short circuit that was responsible for the smoke.

Herbert Hoover declined to chat during the ride to the Capitol for FDR's swearing in.

INAUGURATION 1977

Four days of pageantry, ceremony, and just plain fun

by WILLIAM BARRY FURLONG

The climax, and the *raison d' etre,* of all that took place in the inauguration week was a brief moment in the bright sunshine on January 20. For weeks beforehand the planning covered every detail from how to repair a bandura—an instrument used by a Ukrainian folk singing group—to how to house the horses (there were 340 of them, from Lipizzans to cavalry). "We're trying to give Mr. Carter what he wants—a simple, modest, inexpensive inauguration that will involve all the 215 million people of this country," said Bardyl Tirana, co-chairperson with Vicki Rogers of the 1977 Presidential Inaugural Committee. Some 300,000 invitations had been mailed out. Those who weren't exactly invited decided to come anyway. "Jimmy wants me to come, so I'm coming," said a man from Kentucky. A farmer from Iowa, Elmer Carlson of Audubon, hired some buses and brought 600 of his closer friends to Washington. Then he hired a ballroom and threw parties on three nights for people who couldn't get into official inaugural parties. He figured the expenses at around $100,000

Above, the Carters arrive, parcels and all, January 19. Opposite, Mall fireworks the preceding evening.

but he thought maybe it was worth it.

Of course, there was a little nervous clearing-of-the-throat when Jimmy Carter insisted on having a "People's Inaugural." Some old hands in Washington pointed out that when Andrew Jackson tried it, so many people came to Washington that they had to sleep on pool tables after the hotel beds were all occupied—usually with five to a bed. But then there has always been tut-tutting about inviting the people to the inaugural. When Thomas Jefferson opened up the executive mansion to inaugural visitors for the first time, a diplomat from Europe sniffed patronizingly at the whole affair. He noted that "jingling of a few fifes and drums finished the day. There was nothing dignified in the whole affair."

There was more than the "jingling of a few fifes and drums" at Jimmy Carter's inaugural. There were, in fact, some 200 different musical events on the schedule—brass concerts, classical music, jazz festivals, organ recitals, country and western music, folk music from all over the world. That was only a faint shadow of the entire structure of the festivities. There were prayer

83

Inaugural week began in a near record cold snap, but children watching Ice Follies skaters Tuesday at the National Archives, above and right, barely noticed.

Aaron Copland, above, conducts the National
Symphony in Tuesday's concert, which also featured
Robert Shaw, at left, with the Atlanta Symphony.

Indian dancers in the Union Station Folk Concert.

Ukrainian singers, also at the Union Station Concert.

meetings and poetry readings, parades
and plays, films and fireworks. There
were twelve events especially for children, a half-dozen free tours, and
countless parties and receptions. And
that was only the official list. Un-
officially, there was everything from
the first public showing of the art of
George Meany (the head of the AFL-
CIO, who has been an amateur artist
for 20 years) to a quiet little reception,
instigated by Jimmy Carter, for all
living recipients of the Congressional
Medal of Honor.

The most formidable single factor
surrounding the inauguration week
was the daunting cold. As it happens,
this was something that the inauguration visitors were sharing with the
rest of the country. In Roseau, Minnesota, the temperature dipped to 36
degrees below zero. In Cincinnati, it
was 24 below. In Indianapolis, it was
20 below, and in Pittsburgh and To-
ledo and in Jefferson City, Missouri,
it was 15 below. Even Plains, Georgia,
reported some snow, and the Hudson
River was frozen over, bank to bank.

But in Washington, the cold was
not only unusual but terribly frustrating. The sidewalks were crusted
with hard ice; people in the neighbor-
hoods walked down the streets because they didn't dare walk on the
sidewalks. Some 200 soldiers with
jackhammers were to work cracking
the ice on Pennsylvania Avenue in
time for the parade. The concert on
the Mall, on the first evening, had to
be canceled; the mouthpieces of the
brass instruments would have stuck to
the musicians' lips. And one of the
trains that pulled into Union Station
was out of food, out of coffee, out of
booze, and the passengers couldn't get
off the train for several hours. The
doors had frozen shut.

Cars crept slowly along the ice-
rutted streets in front of the Museum
of African Art on A Street, Northeast,
just a block or so behind the U.S.
Supreme Court building. Inside was a
"small concert" of African music—the

Mikki Ehrenfeld

James Howard Pickerell

Vice President and Mrs. Walter F. Mondale played host
to dignitaries and to friends from Minnesota at receptions
Wednesday in the elegant old Pension Building, right. Below,
the Mondales chat with Bardyl Tirana, inaugural committee
co-chairperson, left, Shirley Temple Black, and others.

Pickerell

playing of gimbeh drums. They are shaped like large toadstools. Their heads are covered with goat skin. And they are tuned with a hammer. But in the hands of the skilled, they can produce a wondrous mixture of sounds and syncopation: all the sounds of west Africa—of Mali and Sierra Leone, of Mauretania and Guinea, of Nigeria and Liberia, of the Upper Volta and Gambia, and Senegal. "It is deep and complicated," said Aristede Pereira of Senegal. Some of the sounds are for funerals, some are for the dance of Chewara ("asking God to fertilize the land"), some are for weddings and baptisms and some are for the joy of man. "The last one we played," said Aristede Percira, "is when we believe something very good is going to happen."

Then next to a complex discipline as dramatic and familiar as a hoe-down. The place was Kennedy Center, elegantly lit, dramatically decorated—red carpeting, red upholstery, off-white walls in the Concert Hall—and dramatically attended: some of the listeners were tie-less, some were in white tie and tails, some were in ruffled shirts and some came in bulky, down-filled jackets and carrying attache cases. Tonight there was not one but two symphony orchestras—the National Symphony conducted by Aaron Copland, then the Atlanta Symphony (and the chorale) conducted by Robert Shaw.

The music was as free and varied as America itself. But Copland, perhaps the greatest living American composer, gave life and vibrancy to his own work: on the "Hoe-Down" from "Rodeo" the 76-year-old composer bounced up and down on the podium like a square dancer. Shaw led the Atlanta Symphony through the familiar tones and undertones of Ives and Gershwin before concluding the concert in an eruptive version of Beethoven's Ninth Symphony. The audience leaped to its feet with cheers and demands for an encore.

Why had Shaw chosen Beethoven and his Ninth for a peculiarly American festival?

all Ken Regan, Camera 5

The inaugural concert at the Kennedy Center, opposite, January 19, was a dazzlingly eclectic array of American dramatic, comic, and musical talent. On this page, from top, Shirley MacLaine, Clamma Dale and Donnie Ray Albert, and Paul Newman.

"For two reasons," he said. "First of all, Beethoven of all composers is concerned with the liberty and brotherhood of man. And second, because the focus of the campaign was—and I believe the focus of the administration will be—brotherhood and the family of man."

On the eve of the inaugural, the festivities took on another, more subtle dimension. On the surface, things continued as they seemed—with tours, concerts, exhibitions, and receptions. But beneath that veneer ran a deeper and somewhat unexpected feeling.

Consider the gala. Officially known as the inaugural concert and televised by CBS, it was not only laced with the most famous names in show biz but proved to be a monument of production. In the wings were three complete structures-on-wheels. All the musicians had to do was get on the set backstage ("Hop on the barge," said a friend to Loretta Lynn) and it would be pulled onstage—behind dropped curtains—by the stagehands of the Opera House in Kennedy Center. At the very same time, in the opposite wing, there was another complete set made up for the 97 members of the National Symphony Orchestra, so that they could take their places and be settled before going on-camera.

Indeed, the crush of entertainment celebrities was so great that some of the production crew had trouble keeping track of them. ("I don't know who it is and what he does," agonized an assistant director trying to keep track of the cast, "but we're missing somebody.") The rehearsal during the day offered glimpses of them that are rarely seen by the public: John Wayne looking huge—almost alien—in a winter overcoat; Muhammad Ali talking very quietly and reasonably—almost improbably—to a radio interviewer; Leonard Bernstein looking gray and short and—almost unbelievably—a little stout in his white tie and tails; Paul Newman looking gallant as he held a door for a photographer.

But with all of the splendor of the

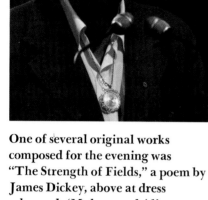

One of several original works
composed for the evening was
"The Strength of Fields," a poem by
James Dickey, above at dress
rehearsal. (Muhammad Ali
contributed a somewhat shorter
work.) Opposite, the Alvin Ailey
dancers present a segment of
Revelations. Below, the Carters
are enjoying the festivities, which
went on way past Amy's bedtime.

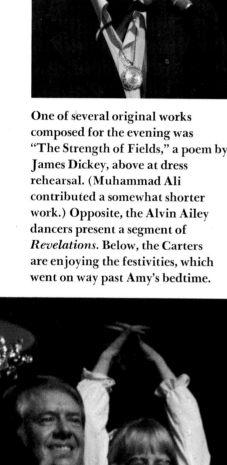

The Strength of Fields

*...a separation from the world,
a penetration to some source of power
and a life-enhancing return ...*
Van Gennep: *Rites de Passage*

Moth-force a small town always has,

Given the night.

What field-forms can be,
Outlying the small civic light-decisions over
A man walking near home?

Men are not where he is
Exactly now, but they are around him   around him like the strength

Of fields.   The solar system floats on
Above him in town-moths.

Tell me, train-sound,
With all your long-lost grief,

what I can give.

Dear Lord of all the fields

what am I going to *do?*
Street-lights, blue-force and frail
As the homes of men, tell me how to do it   how
To withdraw   how to penetrate and find the source
Of the power you always had

light as a moth, and rising
With the level and moonlit expansion
Of the fields around, and the sleep of hoping men.

You?   I?   What difference is there?   We can all be saved

By a secret blooming. Now as I walk
The night   and you walk with me   we know simplicity
Is close to the source that sleeping men
Search for in their home-deep beds.

We know that the sun is away   we know that the sun can be conquered

By moths, in blue home-town air.
The stars splinter, pointed and wild. The dead lie under
The pastures.   They look on and help.   Tell me, freight-train,
When there is no one else
To hear.   Tell me in a voice the sea
Would have, if it had not a better one: as it lifts,
Hundreds of miles away, its fumbling, deep-structured roar
Like the profound, unstoppable craving
Of nations for their wish.

Hunger, time and the moon:

The moon lying on the brain

as on the excited sea   as on
The strength of fields.   Lord, let me shake

With purpose.   Wild hope can always spring
From tended strength.   Everything is in that.
That and nothing but kindness.   More kindness, dear Lord
Of the renewing green.

That is where it all has to start:
With the simplest things.   More kindness will do nothing less
Than save every sleeping one
And night-walking one

Of us.

My life belongs to the world.   I will do what I can.

—*James Dickey*

John Wayne, above, was one of several concert hosts. Below, Leonard Bernstein directs singers and the National Symphony in the new work he dedicated to Rosalynn Carter.

Above, from left at the Kennedy Center, the Carters, Loretta Lynn, Dan Ackroyd with Chevy Chase in a spoof of the swearing-in, Aretha Franklin. Center, House Speaker Thomas O'Neill in the audience with Senator Hubert Humphrey, Bette Davis, Paul Simon, the U.S. Marine Corps Band. Below, Aretha Franklin leads the cast and audience in "God Bless America" to close the show.

Regan

Regan

Rafshoon

Rafshoon

Regan

gala, with all of the radiance of the event, one very subtle but significant point escaped many an onlooker: what other political personage, besides Jimmy Carter, ever got John Wayne and Paul Newman together on the same platform for the same purpose?

Consider another event of the day: the arrival of Jimmy Carter. In history and by tradition, new leaders like to arrive in their capital cities with a certain pomp and grandeur. By way of contrast, Jimmy Carter slipped into town as quietly and unobtrusively as drifting smoke.

There were no bands, no cheering throngs, not even a regal setting. For the President-elect did not arrive at the terminal of Washington National Airport. Instead, his chartered plane rolled up to a vacant space "backstage" at the airport. There were no spectators, only a few reporters, police, cameramen and Secret Service agents. Jimmy got off the plane carrying a bag and a green paper sack, and he helped Rosalynn load the trunk of the chocolate-brown Lincoln Continental that was waiting for him. ("He hates to ride in black limousines," said a newsman somewhat confidentially.) He made only one "statement." It came when the photographers got annoyed at some of Carter's companions on the plane for blocking the view.

"Down in front," called one photographer. Jimmy turned and flashed a big grin.

"Who," he said, "me?"

There were moments which suggested the difference between the public pomp and the private man. When the President-elect arrived at Blair House he took time out to tape an interview for foreign broadcasting on inauguration day. And when he arrived at the gala in formal wear—it was not considered quite the occasion for jeans—he took time, during the intermission, to confer with key aides on the economic package he plans to offer to Congress. Already he was working, though officially he was not yet employed.

Ken Regan, Camera 5

Gerald John Keane

Early January 20, Martin Luther King, Sr., left, presided at Lincoln Memorial, below. Ruth Stapleton, above, the President's sister, also spoke.

Regan

In the predawn hours, the light around the image of Abraham Lincoln was so white, so intense that it seemed almost blue. Until four-thirty in the morning, he was alone in brooding solitude, in the marble monument by the Potomac. One man arrived, then another and another. Fires were built in metal barrels to keep the people warm. It was cold on this morning and it would get colder. At six-thirty, still before the glow rose in the velvety sky to the south and east, two buses pulled up. They were the ushers from the United Nations meditation group who had paid their own way and rode overnight to be here. They came to be "with Abraham"—and to be with history. For here in what was once a muggy swamp hard by the old river, the dawn would rise on a new spirit in the American story.

"Don't be too taken up with *things*," said the old man. The sun was up now and beginning to warm the back between the shoulder blades. The old man had come up here, he said, with "a bit of reluctance and temerity." Years earlier, his son, Martin Luther King, Jr., had stood on these same steps and cried out, "I have a dream." Now the dream passed to other people in another generation. In minutes the prayer service on the Lincoln Memorial would end. In four hours, the new President would mount a different pulpit—this one in front of the Capitol of the United States—take the oath of office and say:

"You have given me a great responsibility—to stay close to you, to be worthy of you, to exemplify what you are.... Your strength can compensate for my weakness, and your wisdom can help to minimize my mistakes.... The American dream endures."

The day of inauguration was cold and clear. It was a day of the people as well as the President. They came to the Capitol in every way possible, by cab, by car, by bus (the inaugural committee chartered 377 buses at a cost of $170,000) and by foot. One woman got to the grounds of the Capitol at four

The Carters, above, are outside the First Baptist Church in Washington, where they and the Mondales attended services as inaugural day began.

The two youngest Carters were up early on the great day. Above, Jack Carter with son Jason, and at right Amy with Rosalynn and Jan Williams, her teacher.

On the steps of the Capitol at midday (opposite), the new President delivered his inaugural address (for a similar, earlier view, see page 77). Clockwise from upper left, Rosalynn Carter and Joan Mondale arrive; Chief Justice Warren Burger administers the oath; Carter thanks his predecessor for "helping to heal our land" (Jeff Carter is in the background); and Lillian Carter, with Mrs. Nelson Rockefeller, looks on.

James Howard Pickerell

Mikki Ehrenfeld

A twenty-one gun salute (below, opposite) brought the inaugural to a close; thousands of people had witnessed the ceremony. Above, the President and his mother lunch at the Capitol; below President Ford bids farewell to the crowd as he prepares to board a helicopter and depart.

o'clock in the morning and camped out, in a sleeping bag, until the oath-taking at noon.

They came, all of them, bearing pride and sometimes a badge—of whimsy or authority. One middle-aged man lurched by the eastern border of the Capitol, wearing a badge that said: "I'm for Carter." Another wore a green badge that said "Official" —green was big on this day, for some of the cars given unlimited access had green placards. But *his* green badge gave him special privileges: in small type it disclosed that the bearer would be "officially" admitted to his country club—and specifically to the bar—during a golf tournament.

They came, all of them, with impressions that were scholarly, or whimsical, or personal. "I understand he's going to lengthen the oath he takes by three words," said one young man in the crush near the entrance to the Capitol grounds.

"How's he going to do that?" said a companion. The official oath, excepting the name, is thirty-five words.

"He's going to get to the end of it and say, 'Y'all hear?' "

The companion trudged on a few steps in silence. Then he said scornfully, "That's two words, not three."

For the people, there were insights and entertainments in the inaugural ceremony that were delightfully unscheduled. They got to hear, for example, what the great men say when they aren't speaking for the public. The reason: the microphones on the podium were "live" and picking up the idle conversation of the participants, though they didn't know it. Mr. Ford, the retiring President, fell into a conversation with Walter Mondale, the Vice President-elect, about Mondale's post-inaugural trip overseas. "Can you sleep on a plane?" asked Mr. Ford. "I don't know," said Mondale, "but we're going to find out." Then later there was the familiar gargle of Nelson Rockefeller, the retiring Vice President, as he sought out Amy Carter, the nine-year-old daughter of the incoming Presi-

Charles M. Rafshoon

Gerald John Keane

99

James Howard Pickerell

dent. "I just wanted to shake your hand. I've heard an awful lot about you, honey," he said.

From one perspective, largely in profile, the President seemed alone as he stepped forward to utter his inaugural speech. For the friends and officials assembled in the background could not be seen from the side and the symbol of the loneliness of the Presidency was etched in the memory like an engraving in time.

"The American dream endures," said the President. "We must once again have faith in our country—and in one another. I believe America can be better. We can be even stronger than before."

When it was over, there were moments of confusion and frustration. The President and his family went inside the Capitol to have lunch, but the people had to pick their way out of the Capitol grounds. It was not an aimless wandering, not the undisciplined march that found thousands upon thousands of people wandering through and across streets on their way to the Capitol. "You had to have a ticket to get in here," grumbled one man. "Now you have to have a ticket to get out." For the idea was to keep the streets clear for the formation of the parade. This baffled some people: One distinguished-looking lady with an unmistakably southern tone approached an official car and explained she needed help to "get to that pointy-looking building up yonder." Even those in the official party didn't have an easy time of it. "We had a terrible time getting a ride from the Capitol," said Hamilton Jordan, the President's assistant.

The parade will be remembered less for its diversity—170 marching units with 15,000 persons—than for its surprise: the President and his family got out of their black limousine and walked the one and a half miles from the Capitol to the White House.

It was a day of work as well as ceremony, of small detail as well as high emotion. At 3:43 P.M., after the parade was over, President Carter and his

The Carters lead the parade.

Some 15,000 people took part in the inaugural parade.
Opposite, the Brentwood High School Band from Long Island
comes up the avenue; above, a pom-pom contingent; at right,
bundled-up sideliners; and below, the theme float, *You Are America.*

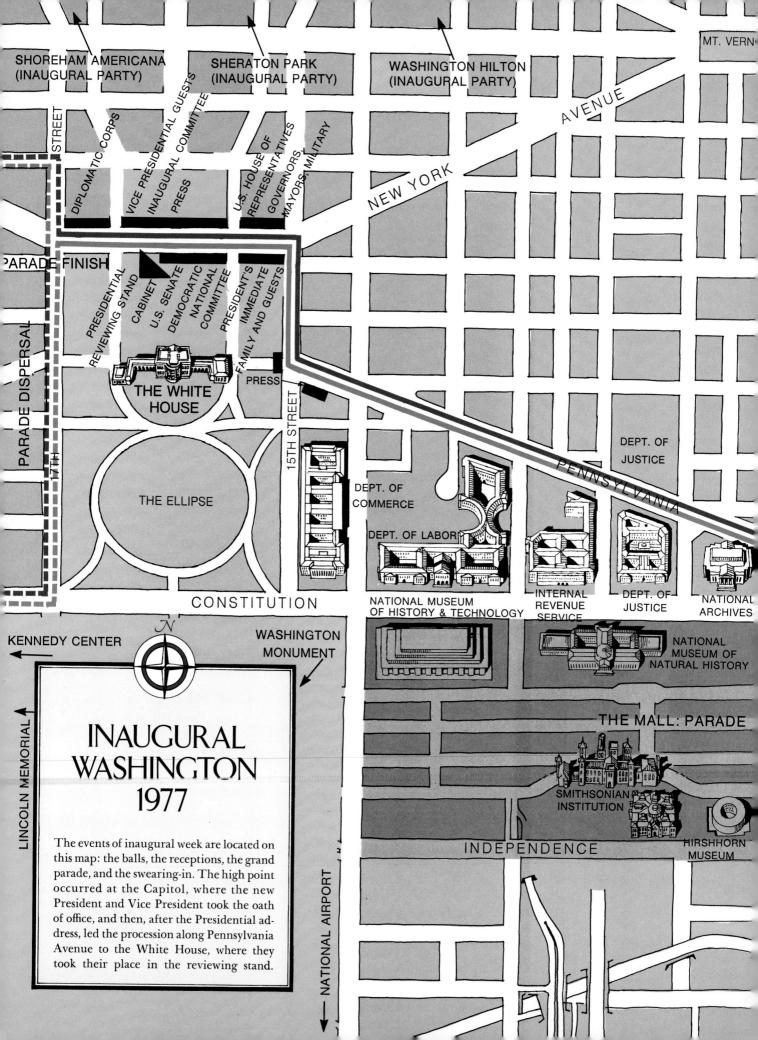

SHOREHAM AMERICANA
(INAUGURAL PARTY)

SHERATON PARK
(INAUGURAL PARTY)

WASHINGTON HILTON
(INAUGURAL PARTY)

MT. VERN

STREET

NEW YORK

AVENUE

DIPLOMATIC CORPS
VICE PRESIDENTIAL GUESTS
INAUGURAL COMMITTEE
PRESS

U.S. HOUSE OF REPRESENTATIVES
GOVERNORS
MAYORS, MILITARY

PARADE FINISH

PRESIDENTIAL REVIEWING STAND
CABINET
U.S. SENATE
DEMOCRATIC NATIONAL COMMITTEE
PRESIDENT'S IMMEDIATE
FAMILY AND GUESTS

PARADE DISPERSAL

17TH

THE WHITE HOUSE

PRESS

15TH STREET

PENNSYLVANIA

DEPT. OF JUSTICE

THE ELLIPSE

DEPT. OF COMMERCE

DEPT. OF LABOR

CONSTITUTION

NATIONAL MUSEUM
OF HISTORY & TECHNOLOGY

INTERNAL REVENUE SERVICE

DEPT. OF JUSTICE

NATIONAL ARCHIVES

KENNEDY CENTER

N

WASHINGTON MONUMENT

NATIONAL MUSEUM OF NATURAL HISTORY

LINCOLN MEMORIAL

INAUGURAL WASHINGTON 1977

The events of inaugural week are located on this map: the balls, the receptions, the grand parade, and the swearing-in. The high point occurred at the Capitol, where the new President and Vice President took the oath of office, and then, after the Presidential address, led the procession along Pennsylvania Avenue to the White House, where they took their place in the reviewing stand.

NATIONAL AIRPORT

THE MALL: PARADE

SMITHSONIAN INSTITUTION

HIRSHHORN MUSEUM

INDEPENDENCE

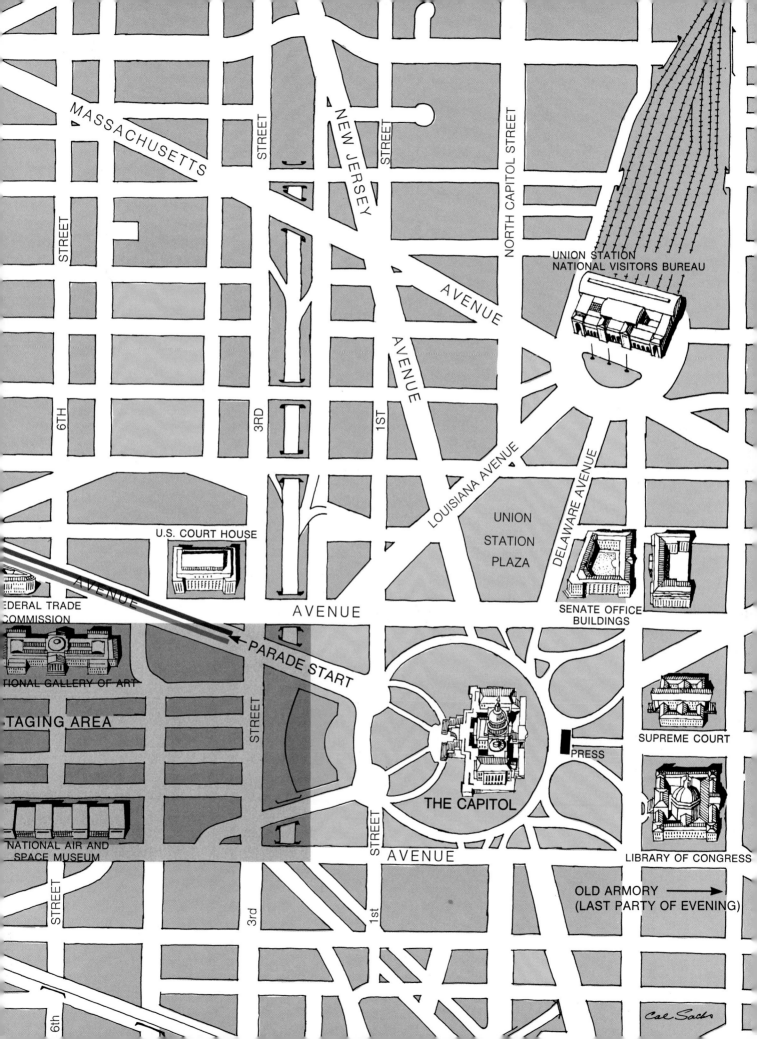

wife wandered across the white waste-land of the grounds of the White House to the north portico. They found that their good friends had preceded them. Some fifteen of Rosalynn's friends from Georgia had come to the Blue Room and the East Room, the Green Room and the Red Room, and decorated them with tu-lips, camellias, snapdragons, poppies, roses, and greens. ("Rosalynn," said one, "will be ecstatic.") Within an hour, the President went to the west wing, and again found that his staff had preceded him. Jody Powell, the press secretary, had walked around shoeless and built a fire in his office.

The yellow and rose Oval Office looked a bit bare, so a secretary had gotten some books to put on the desk. (The books: several volumes of *The Life and Letters of Woodrow Wilson*, and the *Papers of Alexander Hamilton*, volumes V through VII.) There was, on the desk, the inevitable and invariable first sheet to be examined: "The President's Appointments for the Day." (There were four appoint-ments. The first was with Hamilton Jordan. The others were with present and former officials from the various states.) In fact, the Presidency was al-ready a working, functioning organ-ism. President Carter had already signed his first papers while at the Capitol. In room S-208, he had signed the document officially nominating a number of his associates to their Cab-inet-level jobs. A senior staff meeting was held at 4:30 P.M. in the Roosevelt Room, just a few steps away from the Oval Office.

There was to be one more outburst of pleasure and ceremony: the inau-gural parties. There were seven of them; the seventh had to be added because all the tickets to the first six parties had been sold. The rush of the crowds was remorseless. One woman said it had taken her three hours to get a cab. Some people felt it would be easier to walk to the parties through the icy streets. One couple—she in a long gown and furs, he in for-mal wear—were struggling tentatively

Ken Regan, Camera 5

Regan

More than 170 units passed by the White House reviewing stand, below. At left, woodwinds, and above, a unicyclist from Chardon, Ohio. At right, South Carolina's float—a puffing locomotive.

James Howard Pickerell

Regan

What must have been an especially high moment for former Midshipman Jimmy Carter came when the Midshipmen's Corps from Annapolis passed in review (mirrored in the glass front of the Presidential reviewing stand). Admiral James L. Holloway, III, Chief of Naval Operations, salutes at far left as the Carters and the Mondales look on.

109

Charles M. Rafshoon

On inaugural night it took seven parties to accommodate the celebrants. The President and Vice President and their wives stopped in at each. At left, Amy (carrying a book, in case the balls got boring) sets off from the White House with her parents, who appear below at the Washington Hilton. Opposite, from the top, the Union Station ball; a Union Station reveler with triumphal T-shirt; and the Armory party.

Regan, Camera 5

Rafshoon

Mikki Ehrenfeld

"I KNOW, THERE
IS GONNA BE
A CHANGE
I HELPED ELECT
THE MAN FROM
PLAINS"

James Howard Pickerell

over the ice towards the Washington Hilton. "How much farther is it?" she asked. His response was very controlled and very cheerful. "Only nine more blocks," he said.

President Carter attended all the balls. So did his family, but Amy took precautions against getting bored during the dull adult parts: she brought along a book from the White House library—*The Mixed-up Files of Mrs. Basil E. Frankweiler* by E. L. Konigsburg. But there was hardly time to get bored—it all went too fast.

The party at the Sheraton Park Hotel was, perhaps, a microcosm of all seven. There was virtually no breathing room, much less dancing room, in the silver-tinseled ballroom. When Jimmy Carter arrived and approached the microphone, there was a surging from the crowd.

"Are you having a good time?" he asked. The cheers said "yes."

"Are you having a good day?" he asked. Again the cheers.

"Do you believe in America?" he asked. The sound, if possible, grew louder.

"Are you going to help me?" The response was a roar that seemed likely to shatter the mirrored tetrahedrons in the ceiling.

Then, with a phrase, he calmed them down again. "I hope you-all have a good time now," he said. "Because I'm going to dance with my wife."

And then he and Rosalynn stepped off into a stately waltz.

When he was gone, the effect lingered on. "It was beautiful, really beautiful," said a young campaign worker from Youngstown, Ohio, near tears. "Like, 'yeah, we helped put you here and we'll help you do your thing'."

Jimmy Carter had set a fast pace that night. He was early for every party, and he was early getting home —at 12:40 in the morning. He would be up at seven the next day. For there was work to be done.

And he had a working commitment —to the dream that endures.

"Are you having a good time?" was the President's greeting as he and Rosalynn progressed from one inaugural ball to another. "Do you believe in America? Are you going to help me?" The responses were decidedly, even deafeningly, affirmative. Opposite and below, the Carters and the Mondales pay their respects to the crowd assembled at Union Station.

In the long campaign for the nomination and the office, Jimmy Carter and his family traveled nationwide, usually accepting local hospitality for overnight stays. To repay these many kindnesses, the Carters invited some 400 families to the White House January 21. On this page they embrace old friends and, at right, Rosalynn is momentarily overcome. Opposite: the Carters and the Mondales at the governors' reception the same day.

THE SOUTH
AND THE NATION
ARE JOINED

And in good time, too, according to this Southern writer, who envisions a better day for the whole nation

by H. BRANDT AYERS

The pain was so old that it had almost become a friend, a point of reference that Southerners used to define their relationship with each other and to the rest of the nation. It had become almost a physical presence, a door shut at Appomattox that kept us in the comfortable, familiar, and safe rooms within—secure against the uncertainties outside. We leaned against it for support. Then, on the morning of November 3, 1976, it was yanked open. We lurched outside. How would we behave? What did it portend for the nation? What was the state of my own feelings about having a Southern President?

For me the campaign wasn't like the Kennedy-Nixon race when my generation was young. We felt that the elegant Yankee's election or defeat would decide whether everything was possible, or nothing. That old feeling, which was murdered in Dallas, could not be repeated in 1976. But during the last week of the campaign, when Jimmy Carter seemed to be slipping, I found myself caring more than I thought I had. A conversation at that university of common wisdom, the Courthouse Barber Shop, in Anniston, Alabama,

haunted me. One of the seminarians had remarked during the primaries, "If 'they' take the nomination away from Carter, they'll never let us live it down. It'll be another hundred years before any Southerner has a chance." On the Sunday before the election I was reassured by a bit of political intelligence from the rural community of Rabbittown. Outside his trailer home a friend told me, "Most folks around here are going to vote for Carter. They think he knows what it is to put in a day's work. He come up the hard way; he knows what life's all about."

On one level, my Rabbittown friend was saying that he understood the experiences that formed Jimmy Carter's character because they were kin to his own experiences and those of his neighbors. Carter has the common sense that the country needs. But the barbershop seminarian was talking about the deeper meaning of the Carter candidacy—our old friend, scorn: the closed door.

To understand the average Southerner's feelings (and perhaps even more the Southern intellectual's feelings) about a Southern President, it is necessary first to understand the one thing that has made the South different. It wasn't the Civil War, although that is part of it—to know that defeat is possible. We've had one hundred and eleven years to get over that. Neither is it a feeling for the land and a sense of smalltown community. That is part of it, too, but is not unique to the South. There are plenty of friendly Midwesterners who live in small towns with an affinity for the land and each other.

America never thought to look at the entire Middle Western region with scorn or amused condescension. New England never heard the nation, with terrible consistency, speak of its people with sarcasm—heavy words, spoken lightly, cheaply, but so crushing to the spirit. Whether we were black or white, there were words for us and none of them beckoned us to partnership in the national enterprise, or uplifted our soul. We listened to the same radio programs and laughed at our own foibles because there was an element of truth in the caricatures of Amos n' Andy and in the red-necked Lum and Abner's world, the Jot 'Em Down Store.

The old injury, our constant companion, drew us together in a kind of corporate communion, more instinctive than verbal, from East Texas to Virginia. We didn't have to say anything; we knew each other and knew we were different from those on the outside.

There was a time, during the Roosevelt years, when rich and poor, North and South, we shared the same Depression and the same war. FDR liked us. He told us stories and was even known to sample the explosive liquid brought him in fruit jars by county politicians in Warm Springs, Georgia, not far from Plains. But the old ache came back with a vengeance to white Southerners in the 1950's and 1960's, during the Civil Rights Movement when the courage of Southern blacks made Southern whites struggle with their consciences. Martin Luther King, son and father, both continually proclaimed their Southernness. But social revolution at the cutting edge of change is not a normal environment, one that encourages calm reflection and cool behavior. What made

matters worse was the attitude conveyed to us in our own living rooms by television. It seemed as if the original sin of prejudice had just been discovered and isolated, like some exotic virus that flourishes only in subtropical climates. Most Southern whites, who never committed nor considered committing any atrocities, who were trying to adjust to the new ways, got pretty fed up with the adjectives applied to them in their own living rooms.

Then, on the morning of November 3, 1976, the door suddenly opened. We came stumbling out. When the weight was finally lifted, naturally enough there was some jubilation; some hallelujahing and some echoes from the Amen corners. In one corner Eli Evans, the expatriate North Carolinian and foundation executive, whooped at friends across New York traffic. "Free at last!" he shouted. "Free at last. Thank God Almighty; we're free at last."

Unfortunately, the human soul cannot sustain joy; it burns out at the moment of ecstasy. As the days and weeks passed after that brief spasm of elation, a quieter sensation spread warmly through the soul of the region—a sense of confirmation, validation. It was like the awareness of some rural Mississippi boy reviewing his freshman year at Harvard, no longer terrified by the place, knowing he could compete and beginning to think about the responsibilities that would come with his attainments.

That sensation was evident when the Southern governors, legislators, businessmen and scholars gathered at Boca Raton, Florida, in December, to discuss the future of the economy, the nation's and the region's. The Southerners engaged in serious talk and the tone was set by that good and decent man Reubin Askew of Florida. In his keynote address Governor Askew expressed the unspoken agreement among consequential men and women of the South that it is no longer necessary to starve the imagination by feeding it the retarding myths of the past. It is not a time for recalling old wounds but for a positive reconstruction of national will.

Where does the South look to find the language of détente with our separated brothers in the Northeast and Middle West? Edmund Burke's speech, "On Conciliation with America," is a good place to start. That speech, made on March 22, 1775, is one of the enduring political documents of the English-speaking world. Perhaps being a son of defeated Ireland—an indignity fresh and hurtful in the minds of his father and grandfather—Burke did not see things exclusively from the perspective of his adopted island, Invincible England.

"Nothing less will content me than WHOLE AMERICA," he said. "I do not choose to consume its strength along with our own; because in all parts it is the British strength that I consume ... I do not choose wholly to break the American spirit; because it is the spirit that has made the country." There are better remembered lines from that speech, but his rejection of force as a self-cannibalizing tactic is most appropriate now.

From its great oral tradition the South might find the words to use like a poultice to drain poisonous tension from debate, to suspend hostilities by telling a story that creates simultaneous laughter and understanding. Sam Ervin was in that tradition. I remember the old Senator, merry and wise as a country squire, debating with Senator Paul Douglas of Illinois one afternoon. I remember Douglas, prowling the Senate floor like an ancient bear, refusing to accept Ervin's point, and Ervin responding: "The junior Senator from Illinois puts me in mind of an old justice of the peace in Bertie County. If any defendant in his court was represented by counsel he would tell the attorney, 'Son, I'd appreciate it if you wouldn't make any argument in this case because I find that when I hear two sides of an argument it tends to confuse me.' " The nation will be hearing more from Southerners, in and out of government; it could be a welcome change.

One evening at Harvard, where I was a miserable and unlettered lump of red clay from Alabama studying as a Nieman Fellow, I was invited to join the Kennedy Fellows, who were being addressed by the staff director of the Kerner Commission. That was the commission that studied the causes of the urban riots and reported that America was a sick and racist society. It struck me that if that was so, we weren't worth saving. So, I asked, "How do you expect the country to react to your charge that everybody in America is a racist?" Seconds passed. The director said nothing, just stared. I repeated the question, and self-consciously threw in my credentials as a Southern liberal. He looked at me and I felt the room temperature drop. Slowly and deliberately he said, "I understood the question the first time."

My friend James Tinsley wouldn't treat anybody like that, partly because he's older and has seen a lot, but also because he's Southern and black. Once Mr. Tinsley was involved in a discussion of equal opportunity in the hiring and appointment of blacks to city boards. Tension had been building up among the members of the bi-racial committee when Mr. Tinsley began to talk:

You-all put me in mind of the fellow up in Virginia who was makin' rabbit sausage. He got so he was makin' more and more of that rabbit sausage, shippin' it all the way to Texas. It got one fellow to thinkin' and he asked, "It takes a whole lot of rabbits to make all that sausage; where you get all them rabbits?"

The sausagemaker said, "Don't you worry, there's plenty of rabbits."

The other fellow asked, "You sure you don't put anything else in that sausage?"

"Yeah," answered the sausage man, "we put a little something else in it."

"What?"

"A little horse meat."

"How much?"

"Equal parts," answered the sausage man. "Every time we put in a rabbit, we put in a horse."

Mr. Tinsley was as concerned about racism as the Kerner Commission staff director, but he said so in a kindlier way.

Stories like Mr. Tinsley's are verbal evidence of a mind and heart instructed by living among people, as Jimmy Carter has most of his life, who say, "I don't have much, but I have my self-respect." Growing up in Plains, Jimmy Carter absorbed this knowledge, which he learned by attending so many baptisms, weddings, and funerals in the same place, among people that didn't change all that much because they were sons and daughters of sons and daughters he knew, and who knew him. He learned in that tiny Georgia village, with fewer people than a big-city apartment building, to wage the politics of self-respect.

He acknowledged the prevailing courage and pride of black people, even before he hung the portrait of Martin Luther King, Jr., in the Georgia statehouse. Some say that ceremonial act was cynical, political. Surely he was not unaware that the gesture would be noted with approval in a national political campaign, a race he had already decided to run. But a good test of the sincerity of his politics of self-respect is that he did not celebrate the black man at the expense of those who are rural and white. He spoke about that while flying back from the convention:

It's not right to stigmatize people. . . . "All of you are wrong. You shouldn't have done what you did. I'm better than you are." The point I'm making is that the South, including Georgia, has moved forward primarily because it hasn't been put into the position of having to renounce itself. You've got to give people credit for the progress they make and the changes in their attitudes. It would be easy to sit around and say, "Look at those terrible people in Georgia who don't want to bus their kids to school." But that doesn't do any good.

The politics of self-respect says that sorry folks don't come in just one color but that most people, black or white, are normally a lot better than their leaders. Mr. Tinsley and my friend from Rabbittown, the black man and the white man, are united by a shared perception of the same leader. The election returns will not support a leap to the conclusion that the entire country sees the new President just as the two Alabamians do. But those men understand the politics of self-respect, see that is is rooted in the integrity of earth and sweat; and perhaps some of those who in other parts of the nation do not yet believe will understand in time.

Millions of people living, often fearfully, always obscurely, in the nation's older cities need to hear a language of welcome, to hear words that are familiar to them and that communicate a sense of belonging and self-worth. It is a feeling Southerners like Jimmy Carter know. Southerners, black and white, know how it feels to be outsiders, misunderstood and maligned. If President Carter and the other Southerners joining the government at policy levels can communicate their understanding to the urban dispossessed, it would at least give the ethnic minorities of the cities a feeling that they are not alone in their struggle to gain possession of their lives.

There will be more Southerners in Washington because it is natural for the new President to bring with him a cadre of people whose character, intelligence and loyalty he has tested. The transition teams were peopled with Southerners. When fresh talent is poured into the second, third, and fourth echelons of government, it is likely to change both the institution and the pool somewhat.

I do not expect any revolution just because Southern hands seize the throttle of the engine of state. For one thing, it isn't run like an engine. The government has no switches and levers to turn it on and off, no gauges to measure its speed or internal heat. A bureaucratic state is more like a river. It can be dammed and thrown off course but it will find its way around or through the dam. Government can be reorganized, but it cannot be turned at right angles.

The best I can hope for is that government may change its attitudes. And that would be something. Many of those entering government, down to the deputy assistant secretary level and deeper, have had their characters formed in ways similar to that of Jimmy Carter. His family has lived on the same land since 1830. "The passion for home, family, land and stability is strong throughout this region," Roy Reed wrote recently in the *New York Times Magazine.* "The reason is no secret. The South is not only old by most American standards, it is also rural. The rural mentality seeks permanence, however tempted it is by the passing fancy."

Man is more vulnerable before nature, and in

the small towns he is more immediately and directly accountable to his neighbors. Backgrounds like Carter's equip people to resist flattery and even to stand upright in the face of the stiff breezes that may blow from the press. When a high government official goes home to a small town and runs into a farmer on whose fields he has hunted quail, the farmer is not awed by the policy maker's imperial title or his temporary power. He asks, "Where you been, boy?" And the policy maker remembers who he is. A government made up of enough people like that will surely be willing to answer its mail and return its phone calls.

Even before the nation began to refer to the farmer from the Georgia Black Belt as President-elect, there had been some profound changes in the way America saw the new talent pool, the American South. Just as the nation is discovering virtues there that it had not seen before, Southerners themselves are soon likely to change their assumptions about themselves and their role in the nation. We may see this by a remark made in an unlikely place, the oak-paneled office of a corporate board chairman on the eightieth floor of the Empire State Building. This man saw a new class emerging with Carter. "The South is going to produce the new American aristocracy," he told me. Of course, he was not talking about lilac-scented dandies. He was talking about the birth of a new Southern public service establishment, a new legion of national leaders arising from the Lazarus South.

My father was born in 1885. Yet, neither he nor his father could recall a time when our leadership did not come mainly from the men and institutions of the East, nor can I. There was an assumption that Harvard, Yale and Princeton were trade schools for American government and diplomacy. An occasional Southerner might slip into the Executive Branch, especially if he had been laundered first at Princeton. But there was no similar assumption that the graduates of Vanderbilt or Chapel Hill were destined for executive posts in domestic and foreign affairs as a matter of birthright.

Fate, whether kindly or unkindly, allowed the East a longer period of innocence. Arnold Toynbee said that a boy at Groton, for instance, would have felt as Toynbee himself did during the Diamond Jubilee in England. "Well, here we are on the top of the world, and we have arrived at this peak to stay there—forever! There is, of course, a thing called history, but history is something unpleasant that happens to other people."

However, history finally caught up with the last American innocents and rained two thousand years of experience on them in a single decade: Vietnam, economic decline, urban riots, and the discovery that the sin of prejudice is not exclusive to the warmer climes.

I do not wish to lay the cornerstone for a new myth. There are cynical and corrupt men in high positions in the South and any number of politicians who are unequipped intellectually and morally for leadership. Nor do I mean to imply that all Eastern men and institutions are now to be regarded as second rate. History has already rendered its positive judgment about the Deweys and Lehmans and Roosevelts and Harrimans and Rockefellers.

But the nation should rejoice with the South now that it has ceased its fixation with the paraphernalia of the Lost Cause, broken through the Confederate Curtain, and is rediscovering an older Southern tradition. This emotional breakthrough revives in our third century a legacy from the first, the legacy of James Madison, Thomas Jefferson and John Marshall, whose genius and competitiveness cast the fundamental shape of American democracy.

Our nation today is more complete than it was a decade ago. To be born in the South no longer means being an outsider at birth. The door is open for the generation of my six-year-old daughter, Margaret. We have finally come into full historical maturity with the recognition that neither original sin nor God's truth is the exclusive property of any American tribe. There are no moral pinnacles, no top of the world, no exemptions from history. We are all bound by the common lot of man, for good or ill.

The 1977 Inaugural Committee extends its thanks to the following for their efforts
on behalf of the Inauguration of President Jimmy Carter and Vice President Walter F. Mondale, January 20, 1977.

THE 1977 INAUGURAL COMMITTEE

Bardyl R. Tirana, *Co-Chairperson*
Vicki Rogers, *Co-Chairperson*
Lawrence Kieves, *Executive Director*
I. W. Abel, *President,*
United Steelworkers of America
The Hon. Cecil Andrus, *Governor,*
State of Idaho
Mrs. Dolph Briscoe
The Hon. Yvonne Braithwaite Burke,
Chairperson, Congressional Black Caucus
The Hon. Raul Castro, *Governor,*
State of Arizona
The Hon. Richard F. Celeste,
Lt. Governor, State of Ohio
Sol Chaikin, *President, International*
Ladies' Garment Workers Union
The Hon. Midge Costanza, *Vice-Mayor,*
Rochester, New York

The Hon. C. Douglas Dillon
Alfredo Duran
The Hon. Kenneth Gibson, *Mayor,*
Newark, New Jersey
Nancy Hanks, *Chairperson,*
National Endowment for the Arts
Mrs. W. Averell Harriman
The Hon. Richard Hatcher, *Mayor,*
Gary, Indiana
Carlton Hicks, O.D.
Jesse Hill, Jr.
Muriel Humphrey
Mrs. Milton Jones
Coretta Scott King
Lane Kirkland, *Secretary-Treasurer,*
AFL-CIO

Odessa Komer, *Vice President, United*
Auto Workers of America
C. J. McLin, *Chairperson, Democratic*
Black Caucus of Ohio
Eleanor McGovern
The Hon. Henry Maier, *Mayor,*
Milwaukee, Wisconsin
J. Willard Marriott
Arnold Miller, *President,*
United Mine Workers
Luci Johnson Nugent
Mrs. Robert Pauley
S. Dillon Ripley, *Secretary,*
Smithsonian Institute
John Ryor, *President, National*
Education Association

Mrs. Mary L. Scranton
Albert Shanker, *President,*
American Federation of Teachers
William Siddell, *President,*
United Brotherhood of Carpenters and
Joiners of America
Floyd Smith, *President,*
International Association of Machinists
and Aerospace Workers
Robert Strauss, *Chairman,*
Democratic National Committee
Philip M. Walden
The Hon. Walter Washington, *Mayor,*
Washington, D.C.
Glenn Watts, *President,*
Communication Workers of America

THE 1977 INAUGURAL FINANCE COMMITTEE

Richard L. Kattell,
  Co-Chairman
Gordon Jones, *Co-Chairman*
Bert Lance, *Co-Chairman*
A. Robert Abboud
J. Paul Austin
Ken Bannon

W. T. Beebe
Frank Borman
Andrew F. Brimmer
Ed M. Bronfman
Vincent C. Burke, Jr.
Jake F. Butcher
Alexander Calder, Jr.

Anne Cox Chambers
W. Graham Claytor, Jr.
J. W. Davant
Henry Ford, II
C. C. Garvin, Jr.
Jess Hay
Terry Herndon

Jesse Hill, Jr.
Luther Hodges, Jr.
Arthur Krim
Ralph Lazarus
John Loeb
Donald S. MacNaughton

G. W. Miller
R. B. Pamplin
Ed H. Price
J. Mack Robinson
I. S. Shapiro
Jackson T. Stephens

Robert H. Stewart
Eugene Swearington
Richard Swig
J. C. Turner
Lew R. Wasserman
Milton Wolf

THE 1977 PRESIDENTIAL INAUGURAL HOST COMMITTEE

ALABAMA
Dr. A. G. Gaston
Mrs. Lionel W. Noonan
Dorothy S. Carmichael
ALASKA
Lidia Selkregg
ARIZONA
Eliza Carney
Mr. & Mrs. Eugene Bullock
ARKANSAS
Albert H. Rusher
Mrs. Mary Schroeder
CALIFORNIA
David Cunningham
Philip A. Schaefer
Joseph B. Montoya
George Peppard
Rodney Kennedy-Minott
Robert (Buzz) Pauley
COLORADO
Wellington E. Webb
Henry L. Strauss
CONNECTICUT
Pat (Mrs. John) Bowles
Stan C. Weinberg, Jr.
DELAWARE
Becky Gates

Lee Cassidy
DISTRICT OF COLUMBIA
Lillian Huff
FLORIDA
Athalie Range
Dr. Emmet Ferguson
Hazel Tally Evans
GEORGIA
Mrs. Shirley K. Altman
Bill Hopkins
Joe Andrews
Mrs. Elkin Cushman
HAWAII
Mr. Mino Hirabera
IDAHO
Lloyd Walker
ILLINOIS
Marjorie Benton
Jim Wall
Margaret Standish
INDIANA
William Schreiber
IOWA
Harry Baxter
Chuck Gifford
Sharon Maloney

KANSAS
Louise Brock
Marie Vickers
KENTUCKY
Mr. Tracy Farmer
Mrs. Mary Helen Byck
LOUISIANA
A. Z. Young, *Director*
Mrs. Fran Bussie
Nolan Edwards
MAINE
Harold Pachios
Mr. Joe Hakanson
MARYLAND
Dwight Pettit
James Clark
Mrs. Joy Colegrove
MASSACHUSETTS
James W. Hennigan, Jr.
Faith Sarno
Thomas Menino
Kit Dobelle
John Thimas
MICHIGAN
Sylvia McCollough
Mayor Coleman Young

MINNESOTA
Judy Hamilton
MISSISSIPPI
Walter Bivens
Bernadine Young
Paul Neville
MISSOURI
Norm Champ
MONTANA
Chet Blaylock
Bryant Hatch
NEBRASKA
Joan Masuck
NEVADA
Judge Jon Collins
NEW HAMPSHIRE
Jean Wallin
Miss Lucille M. Kelley
NEW JERSEY
Charlie Walther
NEW MEXICO
Faye Hartell
NEW YORK
Bill Vanden Heuvel
NORTH CAROLINA
Bobby Allen

Jane Patterson
John Winters, Jr.
NORTH DAKOTA
Gary Williamson
OHIO
Warren J. Smith
Paula Richardson
OKLAHOMA
Mr. J. C. Kennedy
Mrs. Ben (Fannie) Hill
Larry Wade
OREGON
Betty Roberts
PENNSYLVANIA
Jack Sullivan
Jo Ann Partridge
Stephen Frobouck
Mrs. Elizabeth Atchinson
RHODE ISLAND
Jack Cummings
SOUTH CAROLINA
J. I. Washington
Laura Cummings
Richard W. Riley
SOUTH DAKOTA
Linda Lea Miller
Mike Richardson

TENNESSEE
Mrs. Frances Fifer
Libba Reid
Bryant Millsaps
TEXAS
John Pouland
Bob Armstrong
UTAH
Mayor Ted Wilson
Kay Christensen
VERMONT
Esther Sorrell
VIRGINIA
John Fishwick, *President*
Sandy Duckworth
Henry Howell
WASHINGTON
Karen Marchioro
Nancy Horgan
WEST VIRGINIA
Mrs. Pat Hamilton
George Mills, III
WISCONSIN
Jeanne De Rose
WYOMING
Chuck Graves

THE 1977 ARMED FORCES INAUGURAL COMMITTEE

INAUGURAL COMMITTEE
M.G. Robert G. Yerks, *Chairman*
R.Adm. Ralph H. Carnahan
M.G. William C. Norris
R.Adm. Sidney A. Wallace
B.G. Calhoun J. Killeen
JOINT EXECUTIVE COMMITTEE
Col. Charles H. Mayhew, *Chairman*

Col. Thomas R. Kelly
Capt. John B. Mallard, Jr.
Col. Donald D. Zurawski
Capt. Thomas L. O'Hara, Jr.
SECRETARIAT
Lt.Col. Francis G. Mathison, *Secretary*
Capt. Roger F. Peters,
  Assistant Secretary

SFC Daniel A. Bieger
SP5 Janet L. Anderson
YN2 Nancy A. Dunlap
ADMINISTRATION
Capt. M. Andrew Hulse, *Adm. Officer*
SFC Manuel Munoz
T.Sgt. Michael Paris

LIAISON OFFICERS
Lt.Col. John D. Smith
Lt.Col. William E. Murphy
Capt. James H. O'Beirne
John J. Province

THE NINETY-FIFTH CONGRESS OF THE UNITED STATES OF AMERICA

ALABAMA
Senators
James B. Allen
John J. Sparkman
Representatives
Jack Edwards
William L. Dickinson
Bill Nichols
Tom Bevill

Ronnie G. Flippo
John Buchanan
Walter Flowers
ARIZONA
Senators
Dennis DeConcini
Barry Goldwater
Representatives
John J. Rhodes
Eldon Rudd

Donald E. Young
ARIZONA
Bob Stump
Morris K. Udall
ARKANSAS
Senators
Dale Bumpers
John L. McClellan
Representatives
Bill Alexander

Bob Stump
Morris K. Udall
Ray Thornton
Jim Guy Tucker
CALIFORNIA
Senators
Alan Cranston
Dr. S. I. Hayakawa
Representatives
Harold T. Johnson

John P. Hammerschmidt
Ray Thornton
Jim Guy Tucker
Don H. Clausen
John E. Moss
Robert L. Leggett
John L. Burton
Phillip Burton
George Miller
Ronald V. Dellums
Fortney H. Stark
Don Edwards
Leo J. Ryan

Paul N. McCloskey, Jr.
Norman Y. Mineta
John J. McFall
B. F. Sisk
Leon E. Panetta
John Krebs
William M. Ketchum
Robert J. Lagomarsino
Barry Goldwater, Jr.
James C. Corman
Carlos J. Moorhead
Anthony C. Beilenson
Henry A. Waxman
Edward R. Roybal
John Rousselot
Robert K. Dornan
Yvonne B. Burke
Augustus F. Hawkins
George E. Danielson
Charles H. Wilson
Glenn M. Anderson
Del Clawson
Mark W. Hannaford
Jim Lloyd
George E. Brown, Jr.
Shirley N. Pettis
Jerry M. Patterson
Charles E. Wiggins
Robert E. Badham
Bob Wilson
Lionel Van Deerlin
Clair W. Burgener

COLORADO
Senators
Gary Hart
Floyd K. Haskell
Representatives
William L. Armstrong
Frank E. Evans
James P. Johnson
Patricia Schroeder
Timothy E. Wirth

CONNECTICUT
Senators
Abraham A. Ribicoff
Lowell P. Weicker, Jr.
Representatives
William R. Cotter
Christopher J. Dodd
Robert N. Giaimo
Stewart B. McKinney
Toby Moffett
Ronald A. Sarasin

DELAWARE
Senators
Joseph R. Biden, Jr.
William V. Roth, Jr.
Representatives
Thomas B. Evans, Jr.

FLORIDA
Senators
Lawton Chiles
Richard Stone
Representatives
Robert L. F. Sikes
Don Fuqua
Charles E. Bennett
Bill Chappell, Jr.
Richard Kelly
C. W. Bill Young
Sam M. Gibbons
Andy Ireland
Louis Frey, Jr.
L. A. Bafalis
Paul G. Rogers
J. Herbert Burke
William Lehman
Claude D. Pepper
Dante B. Fascell

GEORGIA
Senators
Sam Nunn
Herman E. Talmadge
Representatives
Bo Ginn
Dawson Mathis
Jack Brinkley
Elliott H. Levitas
Andrew Young
John J. Flynt, Jr.
Larry McDonald

Billy Lee Evans
Ed Jenkins
Doug Barnard

HAWAII
Senators
Daniel K. Inouye
Sparky Matsunaga
Representatives
Daniel K. Akaka
Cecil Heftel

IDAHO
Senators
Frank Church
James A. McClure
Representatives
George Hansen
Steven D. Symms

ILLINOIS
Senators
Charles H. Percy
Adlai E. Stevenson
Representatives
Ralph H. Metcalfe
Morgan F. Murphy
Martin A. Russo
Edward J. Derwinski
John G. Fary
Henry J. Hyde
Cardiss Collins
Dan Rostenkowski
Sidney R. Yates
Abner J. Mikva
Frank Annunzio
Philip M. Crane
Robert J. McClory
John N. Erlenborn
Tom Corcoran
John B. Anderson
George M. O'Brien
Robert H. Michel
Thomas F. Railsback
Paul Findley
Edward R. Madigan
George E. Shipley
Melvin Price
Paul Simon

INDIANA
Senators
Birch Bayh
Richard G. Lugar
Representatives
Adama Benjamin, Jr.
J. Danforth Quayle
David L. Cornwell
Floyd J. Fithian
John Brademas
Elwood Hillis
David W. Evans
John T. Myers
Lee H. Hamilton
Philip R. Sharp
Andrew Jacobs, Jr.

IOWA
Senators
Dick Clark
John C. Culver
Representatives
Edward Mezvinsky
Michael T. Blouin
Charles E. Grassley
Neal Smith
Tom Harkin
Berkley Bedell

KANSAS
Senators
Robert Dole
James B. Pearson
Representatives
Dan Glickman
Martha Keys
Keith G. Sebelius
Joe Skubitz
Larry Winn

KENTUCKY
Senators
Wendell H. Ford
Walter Huddleston
Representatives
John Breckinridge

Tim Lee Carter
Carroll Hubbard, Jr.
Romano L. Mazzoli
William Natcher
Carl D. Perkins
M. G. Snyder

LOUISIANA
Senators
J. Bennett Johnston, Jr.
Russell B. Long
Representatives
Richard A. Tonry
Corrinne C. Boggs (Lindy)
David C. Treen
Joe D. Waggonner, Jr.
Jerry Huckaby
W. Henson Moore
John B. Breaux
Gillis W. Long

MAINE
Senators
William D. Hathaway
Edmund S. Muskie
Representatives
William S. Cohen
David F. Emery

MARYLAND
Senators
Charles McC. Mathias, Jr.
Paul S. Sarbanes
Representatives
Robert E. Bauman
Clarence D. Long
Barbara Mikulski
Marjorie S. Holt
Gladys Noon Spellman
Goodloe E. Byron
Parren J. Mitchell
Newton Steers

MASSACHUSETTS
Senators
Edward W. Brooke
Edward M. Kennedy
Representatives
Silvio O. Conte
Edward P. Boland
Joseph D. Early
Robert F. Drinan
Paul E. Tsongas
Michael J. Harrington
Edward J. Markey
Thomas P. O'Neill, Jr.
John Joseph Moakley
Margaret M. Heckler
James A. Burke
Gerry E. Studds

MICHIGAN
Senators
Robert P. Griffin
Donald W. Riegle, Jr.
Representatives
John Conyers, Jr.
Carl D. Pursell
Garry E. Brown
Edward Hutchinson
Harold S. Sawyer
Bob Carr
Dale E. Kildee
Bob Traxler
Guy Vander Jagt
Elford A. Cederberg
Philip E. Ruppe
David E. Bonior
Charles C. Diggs, Jr.
Lucien N. Nedzi
William D. Ford
John D. Dingell
Wm. M. Brodhead
James J. Blanchard
William S. Brownfield

MINNESOTA
Senators
Wendell A. Anderson
(to be appointed)
Hubert H. Humphrey
Representatives
Albert H. Quie
Tom Hagedorn
Bill Frenzel
Bruce F. Vento

Donald M. Fraser
Richard Nolan
Bob Bergland
(now Cabinet)
James L. Oberstar

MISSISSIPPI
Senators
James O. Eastland
John C. Stennis
Representatives
David R. Bowen
Thad Cochran
Trent Lott
G. V. (Sonny) Montgomery
Jamie L. Whitten

MISSOURI
Senators
John C. Danforth
Thomas F. Eagleton
Representatives
William Clay
Robert A. Young
Richard A. Gephardt
Ike Skelton
Richard Bolling
E. Thomas Coleman
Gene Taylor
Richard H. Ichord
Harold L. Volkmer
Bob D. Burlison

MONTANA
Senators
John Melcher
Lee Metcalf
Representatives
Max Baucus
Ron Marlenee

NEBRASKA
Senators
Carl T. Curtis
Edward Zorinsky
Representatives
John J. Cavanaugh
Virginia Smith
Charles Thone

NEVADA
Senators
Howard W. Cannon
Paul Laxalt
Representative
Jim Santini

NEW HAMPSHIRE
Senators
Thomas J. McIntyre
John A. Durkin
Representatives
Norman E. D'Amours
James C. Cleveland

NEW JERSEY
Senators
Clifford P. Case
Harrison A. Williams, Jr.
Representatives
James J. Florio
William J. Hughes
James J. Howard
Frank Thompson, Jr.
R. Millicent Fenwick
Edwin B. Forsythe
Andrew Maguire
Robert A. Roe
Harold C. Hollenbeck
Peter W. Rodino, Jr.
Joseph G. Minish
Matthew J. Rinaldo
Joseph A. LeFante
Edward J. Patten
Helen S. Meyner

NEW MEXICO
Senators
Peter V. Domenici
Harrison Schmitt
Representatives
Manuel Lujan, Jr.
Harold Runnels

NEW YORK
Senators

Jacob K. Javits
Daniel P. Moynihan
Representatives
Otis G. Pike
Thomas J. Downey
Jerome A. Ambro
Norman F. Lent
John W. Wydler
Lester L. Wolff
Joseph P. Addabbo
Benjamin S. Rosenthal
James J. Delaney
Mario Biaggi
James H. Scheuer
Shirley Chisholm
Stephen J. Solarz
Frederick W. Richmond
Leo C. Zeferetti
Elizabeth Holtzman
John M. Murphy
Edward I. Koch
Charles B. Rangel
Theodore S. Weiss
Herman Badillo
Jonathan B. Bingham
Bruce F. Caputo
Richard L. Ottinger
Hamilton Fish, Jr.
Benjamin A. Gilman
Matthew F. McHugh
Samuel S. Stratton
Edward W. Pattison
Robert C. McEwen
Donald J. Mitchell
James M. Hanley
William F. Walsh
Frank Horton
Barber B. Conable, Jr.
John J. LaFalce
Henry J. Nowak
Jack Kemp
Stanley N. Lundine

NORTH CAROLINA
Senators
Jesse A. Helms
Robert Morgan
Representatives
Walter B. Jones
L. H. Fountain
Charles Whitley
Ike F. Andrews
Stephen L. Neal
Richardson Preyer
Charles Rose
W. G. Hefner
James G. Martin
James T. Broyhill
Lamar Gudger

NORTH DAKOTA
Senators
Quentin N. Burdick
Milton R. Young
Representative
Mark Andrews

OHIO
Senators
John Glenn
Howard Metzenbaum
Representatives
William D. Gradison, Jr.
Mary Rose Oakar
Charles W. Whalen, Jr.
Clarence J. Brown
Thomas N. Kindness
Thomas L. Ashley
Clarence E. Miller
Samuel L. Devine
Ralph S. Regula
John M. Ashbrook
Douglas Applegate
Charles J. Carney
Donald J. Pease
Thomas A. Luken
Tennyson Guyer
Delbert L. Latta
William H. Harsha
J. William Stanton
John F. Seiberling
Chalmers P. Wylie
Louis Stokes
Charles A. Vanik
Ronald M. Mottl

OKLAHOMA
Senators
Dewey F. Bartlett
Henry L. Bellmon
Representatives
James R. Jones
Theodore M. Risenhoover
Wes Watkins
Tom Steed
Mickey Edwards
Glen English

OREGON
Senators
Mark O. Hatfield
Bob Packwood
Representatives
Les AuCoin
Al Ullman
Robert Duncan
James Weaver

PENNSYLVANIA
Senators
H. John Heinz III
Richard S. Schweiker
Representatives
Michael O. Myers
Robert N. C. Nix
Raymond F. Lederer
Joshua Eilberg
Richard T. Schulze
Gus Yatron
Robert W. Edgar
E. G. Shuster
Joseph M. McDade
Daniel J. Flood
John P. Murtha
Lawrence Coughlin
William S. Moorhead
Fred B. Rooney
Robert S. Walker
Allen E. Ertel
Douglas Walgren
William F. Goodling
Joseph M. Gaydos
John H. Dent
Austin J. Murphy
Joseph S. Ammerman
Mark L. Marks
Gary A. Myers
Peter H. Kostmayer

RHODE ISLAND
Senators
John H. Chafee
Claiborne Pell
Representatives
Edward P. Beard
Fernand J. St. Germain

SOUTH CAROLINA
Senators
Ernest F. Hollings
Strom Thurmond
Representatives
Menel J. Davis
Floyd Spence
Butler Derrick
James R. Mann
Kenneth L. Holland
John W. Jenrette, Jr.

SOUTH DAKOTA
Senators
George McGovern
James Abourezk
Representatives
Larry Pressler
James Abdnor

TENNESSEE
Senators
Howard H. Baker, Jr.
James R. Sasser
Representatives
James H. Quillen
John J. Duncan
Marilyn Lloyd
Albert Gore, Jr.
Clifford R. Allen
Robin L. Beard
Ed Jones
Harold E. Ford

TEXAS
Senators
Lloyd M. Bentsen
John G. Tower
Representatives
Sam B. Hall, Jr.
Charles Wilson
James M. Collins
Ray Roberts
Jim Mattox
Bill Archer
Olin E. Teague
Omar Burleson
George H. Mahon
Robert Krueger
Abraham Kazen, Jr.
Bob Gammage
Jack Brooks
J. J. Pickle

W. R. Poage
James C. Wright, Jr.
Jack Hightower
John Young
E. K. de la Garza
Richard C. White
Barbara Jordan
Henry B. Gonzales
Dale Milford

UTAH
Senators
Jake Garn
Orrin G. Hatch
Representatives
K. Gunn McKay
Dan Marriott

VERMONT
Senators
Patrick J. Leahy

Robert T. Stafford
Representative
James M. Jeffords

VIRGINIA
Senators
Harry F. Byrd, Jr.
William Lloyd Scott
Representatives
Paul S. Trible, Jr.
G. William Whitehurst
David E. Satterfield III
Robert W. Daniel, Jr.
W. C. Daniel
M. Caldwell Butler
J. Kenneth Robinson
Herbert E. Harris II
William C. Wampler
Joseph L. Fisher

WASHINGTON
Senators
Henry M. Jackson
Warren G. Magnuson
Representatives
Joel Pritchard
Lloyd Meeds
Don Bonker
Mike McCormack
Thomas S. Foley
Norman D. Dicks
Brock Adams
   (Cabinet)

WEST VIRGINIA
Senators
Robert C. Byrd
Jennings Randolph
Representatives

Robert H. Mollohan
Hardey O. Staggers
John Slack
Nick Joe Rahall II

WISCONSIN
Senators
Gaylord Nelson
William Proxmire
Representatives
Les Aspin
Robert W. Kastenmeier
Alvin Baldus
Clement J. Zablocki
Henry S. Reuss
William A. Steiger
David R. Obey
Robert J. Cornell
Robert W. Kasten, Jr.

WYOMING
Senators
Clifford P. Hansen
Malcolm Wallop
Representative
Teno Roncalio

D.C.
Delegate Walter E. Fauntroy

GUAM
Delegate Antonio Borja
   Won Pat

PUERTO RICO
Resident Commissioner
   Battasar Corrado Del Rio

VIRGIN ISLANDS
Delegate Ron de Lugo

1977 INAUGURAL COMMITTEE STAFF

John Abernathy
Liz Abernathy
Sandy Abrums
Diane Alnutt
Marti Barrett
Bonni Barnes
Arthur Barth
Mary Lou Batt
Paul Bawol
Tom Beard
Mary Beazley
James E. Beavers
Mary Berkeley
Ruth Berry
Stephen Bittel
Lt. Bruce E. Boevers
Paul Boswell
Mark Brand
Don Brock
Marie Brookter
Alice Bruce
Robert Burke
Stuart Byer
Ron Byrd
Enrique Cancino
Robert Carr
Chet Carter
Jean Carter
Walton Chalmers
Edward Chidakel
Nancy C. Clasen
Gladys Clearwaters
Nancy Coggins
Nancy F. Cole
Jean Coleman
Peter David Conlon
Pattie Conway
Dori Corrado
Rev. James Covington
Delacy Cox
Ann Crites
Kathlyn Crittenden
Bill Cunnane
Rae Dasher
Wayne Dasher
Alma Davis
Doris Dean
Margaret Demere
Jim Denbo
Tom Dawson
Malcolm W. Diggs
Molly Dillon
Don Doll
Bunny Dorsett
Lucille Douglas

Scott Douglass
Jack Dover
K. Drew
Peter Duchin
Becky Dudley
James Dunton
Dan Dwyer
Harron Ellenson
Conora Elliott
Minor Elson
Sarah Lou Erickson
Francis Fitzpatrick
Moira Flanagan
Martin M. Freeman
Nicholas Friendly
Robert A. Gaines
Vicki Gaines
Keith Garland
Mark Gettelson
Andrew Gheetner
Robert Gilson
Ronnie Gold
Kevin Gorman
Gardiner Grant
Fred Gray
Helen Gray
Nancy Greene
Eve Greenfield
Bill Griffis
Thomas Gross
Bob Grossman
Dennis Grubb
Margaret Gudbranson
John Hager
Marilu Halamandaris
Ellie Halley
Mary Hanley
Veronica Harley
Shirley Havrilka
Debbie Hawkins
Stephen Hayes
Sarah Hendrix
Ellen Herman
Debra Hershberg
Cathy Hirsch
Alan Hotchkiss
Cindy Howar
Lt. Julia Hubbel
Lillian Huff
Bill Hudson
Lesley Israel
Marie Jackson
Rolf Jacoby
Claudette Johnson
Jim Johnson

David Joyner
Kathy Joyner
Charline Keith
Jack Kelly
Joan Larson Kelly
Marguerite Kelly
Lorraine C. Kennedy
Jim Kornreich
Gene Kraus
Alice Kravitz
Carmella LaSpada
Jeanne Lee
Dale Leiback
Mac Lipscomb
Andy Litsky
Steve Littleton
Robert Lohse
Lee Lunsford
Cooki Lutkefedder
Bill Mabry
James MacKinnon
Capt. Leslie Magee
Beulah Magruder
David Manley
Mike Mapes
Paulett Marlow
Larry D. McCoy
Michael D. McCray
Martha McGowan
Diane McGuinness
Bill Megaro
Paul Melbostad
Annie Mendoza
Bob Mikkelson
Seth Miller
Bunnie Mitchell
Elizabeth Mitchell
Betty Mizek
Curt Moffatt
Lee Monroe
Cynthia Moore
Pat Moran
A. Z. Morton
Edwena Murphy
Michelle Nelson
Julian Nicholas
Angie Novello
Capt. James H. O'Beirne
Jeannie Offholter
Billie Oliver
Julie Onic
Carl Pace
Dot Padgett
Hardy Patten
Rodney Perlman

Frank Phifer
John Pritchard
John J. Province
Betty Quinn
Wayne Rackoff
Gerald M. Rafshoon
Bill Ramsaur
Laverne Ray
Paige Reffe
Sally Regal
Ralph Rinzler
Jennie Robinson
Ron Robinson
Ellen Rothman
James Rowe
Michelle Runyon
Pinky Rutledge
Debra Sale
Rita Samuels
Dennis Scardilli
David Schmidt
Otto Schmidt
Catherine Scott
Lou Anne Scott
Tricia Segall
S. Steven Selig III
Jo Anne Sharlach
Lee Sheehy
Tom Shelton
Story Shem
A. Z. Shows
Dennis Shumaker
Mary Silkworth
Leonard Silverstein
Steve Simmerman
Wade Skiles
Jack Skuce
Jim Smith
Kristin Smith
Peggy Smith
David Smoak
Wattie Snowden
Patricia Staley
Karen Stall
Dr. Raymond L. Standard
David Stempler
Randall Stempler
Jake Sullivan
Judy Sullivan
Paul Sullivan
Carol Summerour
Paul Suplizio
Woodrow O. Swanson
Mae Sykes
J. Nick Taylor

Helen Taylor
Stan Temple
Rita Thompson
Al Thompson
Gail Tirana
Jo Jo Trued
Vwrry Ruewn
Christine Turpin
John Tyler
Joseph Tyler II
Peggy Tyler
Koko Unger
Marcel Veilleux
Gerald Vento
Gladys Voegtli
Sue Vogelsinger
Wolf Von Eckhart
William Waddell
Noreen Walsh
Ervin Webb Jr.
Rob Weeks
Mark S. Weiner
Steve Weinstein
Joseph Weiss
Carol West
Marjorie West
Landon Wilder
Barbara Wiley
Steve Wilkinson
Penny Williams
Salome Williams
Susan Williamson
Clayton Willis
Frank Wilson
Antonia Wood
Denise Wood
Russell Woodman
Edward Woody
Burdette Wright
Ken Wrightman
Diana Wyatt
Rita Yavinsky
Elaine Zessi
Edie Agin
Greg Andrews
Robert Andrews
Ann Baker
Warren Baker
Ruth Barry
John Henry Brebbia
Gudrun Brown
Esther Coopersmith
Mel Cotten
George Cottman

Stephen Creskoff
Jean Davis
Sheryl Dawdy
Lloyd Delvauy
Foresteen Dickerson
Fred Droe
Elizabeth Dudley
A.D. Frazier, Jr.
Maggie Gill
Janet Glen
John Good
George Grandison
Charles Gravely
Bruns Grayson
Mary Hangerud
Ed Heffernan
Larry Herman
Ann Hillman
Diane Huff
Fred Israel
Debbie Jackson
Norma Jackson
Ben F. Johnson
Pat Johnson
Linda Kieves
Lita Lamont
H.H. Leonards
Alicia Levinson
Dale Markley
DeVadia Martin
John G. Martin
Kitty McKenzie
Keith Miles
Ken Nicholas
O'Brien Price
William R. Pollak
Paul Porter
Betty Rainwater
Allan Raychap
Lucille Savage
Lisa Sergio
Donald Skinder
Albert Soto
Sam Starobin
Andy Stein
Curtis Taylor
Betsy Tibbs
Debbie Von Hoffman
James G. Walls
Vernella Watford
Vivian Watts
John P. Wheeler, III
Everett H. Wilcox, Jr.
William C. Wren

CONGRESSIONAL MEDAL OF HONOR RECIPIENTS

Lucian Adams
Stanley T. Adams, Lt.Col. (Ret.)
Beauford T. Anderson
Webster Anderson
Thomas E. Atkins
John P. Baca
Nicky D. Bacon, S.Sgt.
William Badders, Cmm. (Ret.)
John F. Baker, Sgt.
John H. Balch, Cdr. (Ret.)

Donald B. Ballard
William E. Barber, Col. (Ret.)
Van T. Barfoot, Col. (Ret.)
H. C. Barnum, Jr., Maj.
Carlton W. Barrett
Stanley Bender
Edward A. Bennett, Maj. (Ret.)
Gary B. Beikirch, Sgt.
Melvin E. Biddle
Arnold L. Bjorklund, Lt. (Ret.)

David B. Bleak
Orville E. Bloch, Col. (Ret.)
Paul L. Bolden
James L. Bondsteel, S.Sgt.
Gregory P. (Pappy) Boyington
Patrick H. Brady, Lt.Col.
Herschel F. Briles
Maurice L. Britt, Capt. (Ret.)
Paul W. Bucha
John D. Bulkeley, R.Adm. (Ret.)

Francis X. Burke
Lloyd L. Burke, Col.
Herbert H. Burr
James M. Burt
Richard E. Bush
Robert E. Bush
Hector A. Cafferata
Donald Call
Jose Calugas, Capt. (Ret.)
Jon R. Caviani, S.Sgt.

Justice M. Chambers, Col. (Ret.)
William R. Charette
Ernest Childers, Lt.Col. (Ret.)
Clyde L. Choate
Francis J. Clark
R. Mike Clausen, Jr.
Mike Colalillo
James P. Connor
Charles H. Coolidge
Clarence B. Craft
W. J. Crawford, M.Sgt. (Ret.)
John R. Crews
Jerry K. Crump, M.Sgt.
Francis S. Currey
Edward C. Dahlgren
Peter J. Dalessandro
Michael J. Daly
Charles W. Davis, Col. (Ret.)
Raymond G. Davis, Gen. (Ret.)
Sammy L. Davis
George E. Day, Col.
William F. Dean, M.Gen. (Ret.)
Jefferson J. De Blanc, Col. (Ret.)
E. H. Dervishian, Col. (Ret.)
M. H. Dethlefson, Col.
Duane E. Dewey
Drew D. Dix, Capt.
Carl H. Dodd, Maj.
David C. Dolby
Roger H. Donlon, Lt.Col.
James H. Doolittle, Gen. (Ret.)
Desmond T. Doss
Jesse R. Drowley
Kern W. Dunagan, Maj.
Russell Dunham
Robert H. Dunlap, Maj. (Ret.)
Walter D. Ehlers
Henry E. Erwin
Forrest E. Everhart
Frederick E. Ferguson, Capt.
John W. Finn, Lt. (Ret.)
Almond E. Fisher, Lt.Col. (Ret.)
Bernard F. Fisher, Col. (Ret.)
M. J. Fitzmaurice
James P. Fleming, Maj.
Eugene B. Fluckey, R.Adm. (Ret.)
Robert F. Foley, Maj.
Joseph Foss, B.Gen. (Ret.)
Wesley L. Fox, Maj.
Harold A. Fritz, Capt.
Leonard A. Funk
Samuel G. Fuqua, R.Adm. (Ret.)
Harold A. Furlong, Col. (Ret.)
Robert E. Galer, Brig.Gen. (Ret.)
Harold A. Garman
Donald A. Gary, Cdr. (Ret.)
Robert E. Gerstung
Nathan G. Gordon, Lt.Cdr. (Ret.)
Stephen R. Gregg
Charles C. Hagemeister, Maj.
William E. Hall
Pierpont N. Hamilton, M.Gen. (Ret.)
H. H. Hannaken, B.Gen. (Ret.)

Raymond Harvey, Lt.Cdr. (Ret.)
John D. Hawk
George P. Hays, L.Gen. (Ret.)
James R. Hendrix
Frank A. Herda
Rudolfo P. Hernandez
Silvestre Herrera
Rufus G. Herring, Lt.Cdr. (Ret.)
Ralyn M. Hill
Joe R. Hooper
Freeman V. Horner, Maj. (Ret.)
James H. Howard, Br.Gen. (Ret.)
Jimmie E. Howard, 1st Sgt. (Ret.)
Robert L. Howard, Capt.
William R. Huber, Lt. (Ret.)
Thomas J. Hudner, Capt. (Ret.)
Paul B. Huff, Sgt.Maj. (Ret.)
Einar H. Ingman
E. V. Izac, Cdr. (Ret.)
Arthur J. Jackson
Joe M. Jackson, Col. (Ret.)
Jack H. Jacobs, Maj.
Douglas T. Jacobson, Maj. (Ret.)
Don J. Jenkins, S.Sgt.
Delbert O. Jennings, 1st Sgt.
Lawrence Joel, Sgt.F.Cls. (Ret.)
Leon W. Johnson, Gen. (Ret.)
Oscar G. Johnson
William J. Johnston
John R. Kane, Col. (Ret.)
Phillip C. Katz
Benjamin Kaufman
Kenneth M. Kays
Leonard B. Keller
Thomas G. Kelley, Cdr.
Allan J. Kellogg, G.Sgt.
Charles E. Kelly
Thomas J. Kelly
Robert S. Kennemore
Joseph R. Kerrey
Thomas J. Kinsman
Gerry H. Kisters
A. W. Knappenberger
E. R. Kouma, M.Sgt. (Ret.)
George C. Lang
Clyde E. Lassln, Lt.
W. R. Lawley, Jr., Col. (Ret.)
Robert E. Laws
Daniel W. Lee
Howard V. Lee, Lt.Col. (Ret.)
Hubert L. Lee
J. H. Leims, Capt. (Ret.)
Peter C. Lemon
John L. Levitow
Jake W. Lindsey
Angelo J. Litkey
Gary L. Littrell, S.Sgt.
J. E. Livingston, Maj.
James M. Logan
Jose M. Lopez, Sgt.F.Cls (Ret.)
George M. Lowry, R.Adm. (Ret.)
Jacklyn H. Lucas
Allen J. Lynch

George L. Mapry, M.Gen. (Ret.)
Charles A. Mac Gillivary
Walter J. Marm, Maj. (Joe)
Robert D. Maxwell
Melvin Mayfield
David Mc Campbell, Capt. (Ret.)
Joseph J. McCarthy, Col. (Ret.)
Finnis D. McClerry
Richard M. McCool, Capt. (Ret.)
Charles L. McGaha, Maj. (Ret.)
Vernon McGarity
John C. McGinty, Capt.
William L. McGonagle, Capt. (Ret.)
John R. McKinney
A. L. McLaughlin, M.Sgt. (Ret.)
David H. McNerney
John W. Meagher
Gino J. Merli
Edward S. Michael, Lt.Col. (Ret.)
John Mihalowski, Cdr. (Ret.)
Franklin D. Miller
Lewis L. Millett, Col. (Ret.)
Hiroshi H. Miyamura
Ola L. Mize, Lt.Col.
R. J. Modrzejewski, Lt.Col.
Jack C. Montgomery
John C. Morgan
Charles B. Morris, M.Sgt.
Raymond G. Murphy, Capt. (Ret.)
Charles P. Murray, Col. (Ret.)
R. B. Myers, Col. (Ret.)
Ralph G. Nepple
Robert B. Nett, Col. (Ret.)
Beryl R. Newman
Henry N. Nickerson
Thomas R. Norris, Lt. (Ret.)
Michael J. Novosel
George H. O'Brien, Lt.Col. (Ret.)
Carlos C. Ogden
Richard H. O'Kane, R.Adm. (Ret.)
Robert E. O'Malley
Richard H. O'Neill
Nicholas Oresko
Mitchell Paige, Col. (Ret.)
Robert M. Patterson, S.Sgt.
Archie A. Peck
Richard A. Penry
Francis J. Pierce
John A. Pittman
Richard A. Pittman, S.Sgt.
Everett Pope
Thomas A. Pope
L. P. Ramage, V.Adm. (Ret.)
Ronald E. Ray
Gordon R. Roberts
Louis R. Rocco, WO
Cleto L. Rodriguez, M.Sgt.
Joseph C. Rodriguez, Lt.Col.
Charles C. Rogers, M.Gen.
Donald K. Ross, Capt. (Ret.)
Wilburn K. Ross, M.Sgt. (Ret.)
Ronald E. Rosser
Carlton R. Rouh, Capt. (Ret.)

Donald E. Rudolph, M.Sgt. (Ret.)
Alejandro Ruiz
Samuel M. Sampler
Clarence E. Sasser
Joseph E. Schaefer
Henry Schauer
C. F. Schilt, Lt.Gen. (Ret.)
H. E. Schonland, R.Adm. (Ret.)
E. R. Schowalter, Jr., Col.
Robert S. Scott, Col. (Ret.)
William Seach, Lt. (Ret.)
Charles W. Shea, Lt.Col. (Ret.)
William A. Shomo, Lt.Col. (Ret.)
David M. Shoup, Gen. (Ret.)
Franklin E. Sigler
Robert E. Simanek
Carl L. Sitter, Col. (Ret.)
John C. Sjogren, Maj. (Ret.)
Maynard H. Smith
William A. Soderman
Richard K. Sorenson
James M. Sprayberry, Capt.
Junior J. Spurrier
James B. Stockdale, R.Adm.
James L. Stone, Col.
George L. Street, Capt. (Ret.)
Kenneth E. Stumpf, Sgt.F.Cls.
James E. Swett, Col. (Ret.)
James A. Taylor, Maj.
Brian M. Thacker
Max Thompson
Michael E. Thornton, Eng 1/c
Leo K. Thorsness, Col. (Ret.)
John J. Tominac, Lt.
Jack L. Treadwell, Col. (Ret.)
Donald L. Truesdell, CWO (Ret.)
Louis M. Van Iersel
Archie Van Winkle, Lt.Col. (Ret.)
Jay R. Vargas, Maj.
Dirk J. Vlug
Forrest L. Vosler
Reidar Waaler
George E. Wahlen (Ret.)
Kenneth A. Walsh, Lt.Col. (Ret.)
W. D. Watson
Ernest L. West
Gary G. Wetzel
Eli Whiteley (Ret.)
Paul J. Wiedorfer
William H. Wilbur, Br.Gen. (Ret.)
Charles H. Willey
Charles Q. Williams, Maj. (Ret.)
Hershel W. Williams
J. Elliott Williams
Benjamin F. Wilson, Maj. (Ret.)
Harold E. Wilson CWO (Ret.)
Louis H. Wilson, Gen.
Raymond R. Wright
Gerald O. Young, Lt.Col.
Fred W. Zabitosky, 1st Sgt.
Jay Zeamer, Lt.Col. (Ret.)
William Zuiderveld, Lt. (Ret.)

FULL TIME VOLUNTEERS

Elizabeth Abernathy
John Abernathy
Douglas Alpert
Ann Marie Baker
Vi Baluyut
Ann Bauersfield
Paul Bawol
Ellen Berlow
Wes Bersch
Richard Blanks
Deloris Branch
Jane Brenner
Alice Bruce
Jacqueline Bryant
Margaret Bryant
Betty Carraway
Nancy Clasen
Louis Clinton
Nancy Cohen
JoAnn Crites
Alma Davis
Paul Davis

Doris Dean
Louis De Turro
Malcolm Diggs
Kelly Donley
Lucille Douglas
Cheryl Dowdy
Patricia Driscoll
Martin Duggan
David Dunning
Conora Elliott
Sarah Lou Erickson
Guadalupe Espinosa
Elizabeth Evenson
Helen F. Foster
Soussan Gazani
Carol Currie Gidley
Chris Gitlin
Charles Glovee
Alice Godaire
Ronnie Gold
Fred Gray
Helen Gray

Marilyn Guiraud
Rosalie Haley
Lorna Hammes
Mary Hangerud
Denise Harrison
Michelle Hart
Willie Mae Hart
Veronica Harley
Linda Hartke
Michael Hartman
Debbie Hawkins
Ginger Holmes
Lesley Israel
John Jackson
Marie Jackson
Bill Jenkins
Pat Johnson
Kathy Joyner
Joan Kelly
Charles Kemp
Lorraine Kennedy
Judith Lewis

Steve Littleton
Susan Lee Lumsford
Theodore McCormick
Larry McCoy
Martha McGowan
William Mabry
Bill Magaro
Leslie Magee
Beulah Magruder
Cilla Marks
Barbara Martin
Willie Maynard
Marilee Menard
Renee Miller
Lee Monroe
Patricia Moran
Albert Moskowitz
Hubert Neal
Lorenzo Neal
Paul Nickens
Sharon Nickens

Angela Norvello
WillieMae Oliver
Dot Padgett
Cindy Palmer
Helen Parker
Bill Perry
Kevin Phelps
Jo Phillips
Laverne Ray
Ralph Rinzler
Jennie Robinson
Rita Samuels
JoAnne Sharlach
Mary Alice Smith
Nancy Stewart
Jane Stuckert
Kelly Sullivan
Gail Sumpter
Laura Sutherland
Frederick Sykes
Mae Sykes

Ervin Webb
Mark Weiner
Helen Taylor
Frederick Terman
Mary Scott Ternus
Bradley Thompson
John Toole
Jo Trued
Betty Turen
Mary Utz
Gladys Voegtli
Ervin Webb
Mark Weiner
Kelley Weissenborn
Rev. Preston Williams
Frances Williamson
Earline Winkey
Betty Lou Winslow
Antonia Wood
Russell Woodman
Burdette Wright

PART TIME VOLUNTEERS

Roosevelt Adams
Dale Alfonzo

Larry Alkofer
Lisa Alkofer

James Allison
Louis Allison

Cynthia Alston
Deborah Anderson

Jean Anderson
Ruth Anderson

Walter Anderson
Lisa Andes

Susan Anokop
Doreen Arzoomanian
Ann Baekey
Kay Badbezanchi
Barbara Bafford
Lloyd Bafford
Joel Bander
Sandra Barnes
San Louisa Barnes
Verda Barnes
Arthur Barth
Herbert Bass
Marylou Batt
Susan Bayley
Evelyn Beasley
Geraldine Bell
Cynthia Benn
Jeffrey Berg
Joel Bergsma
Evelyn Berrigan
Thomas Bertley
Charlotte Bickett
Sumiko Biderman
Thelma Blackwell
Bobby Bledsoe
Dimity Bledsoe
Joyce Block
Mary Bouers
Freddie Booker
Jane Bosman
Pat Botts
Hyatt Boyette
Mary Boyette
Loretta Bowen
Chip Boylan
Eric Branch
Hazel Brantley
Pam Brewington
Bob Bristow
Travis Britt
Derrick Broadie
Arthur Brodsky
Barbara Brooks
Betty Brooks
Arsula Brown
Irene Brown
Karen Brown
Marilyn Brown
Peggy Brown
Vomcile Brownlowe
Alice Bruce
Jacqueline Bryte
Michael Buake
Jay Buell
Nancy Burke
Sharon Burke
Arlene Burruss
Barbara Butler
Judy Butler
Nancy Cain
Madlyn Calbert
Thomas Callahan
Patsy Callicut
Mary Ann Camp
Grace Cantwell
Virginia Carr
Brenda Carroll
Mary Carrozza
Pat Carter
Avaleen Chadwick
Delia Chapman
Lorna Chappell
Leona Chazen
Linda Chernisky
Clyde Christian
Dorothy Christian
Jean Chybinski
Harriett Cipriani
Vivian Coghlan
Alan Coiro

Elizabeth Coker
Nancy Cole
Christine Coleman
Ferne Collins
Jan Dell Conley
Jackie Cope
Linda Cook
Ed Cooke
Eloise Corry
Viola Covington
William Crawford
Calvin Crawl
Betty Croghan
Katherine Cross
John Crowley
Helen Cunningham
Lynne Curtice
Wayne Dasher
Sarah Daughtridge
Kritini Davenport
Daryl Davis
Debra Davis
Ricardo Davis
William Davis
LuAnne Dawson
Margaret Demere
Richard Diamond
Floresteen Dickerson
Nancy Doten
Jane Duncan
Johnnie Durant
Margaret Durham
Barbara Eck
Michael Eck
Herron Ellison
Minor Elson
Frank Enten
Mabel Evans
Willie Fairell
Margaret Farrar
Michael Felder
Joyce Feldman
Mike Fennell
Susan Fennell
David Ferguson
Judith Ferrera
Betty Fiason
Jay Finkelstein
Sheldon Fisher
Ilissa Flamm
Melvin Fox
Mark Freedenberg
Herman Gaines
Connie Gallogly
Daniel Garcia
Ken Garcia
Leonard Garrett
WillieMae George
Audrey Gibson
Maggie Gill
Bertha Ginyard
Mark Gittelson
Emory Givens
Chris Gladstone
Janet Glen
Mary Glenn
Cynthia Glimpse
Kevin Glover
Linkins Golden
Barbara Goldman
David Goodman
William Goodwin
Henrietta Gould
Alex Grant
Gardiner Grant
June Grant
Kathryn Grant
Evelyn Green
Jacinta Green
Lynnette Green

Barbara Gregory
Mary Gregory
Paul Grice
Bob Grossman
Albert Gueory
Bea Hackett
Sudka Haley
Dorothy Hall
Jeanne Halleck
Paulette Hammond
Eleanor Hansen
Erling Hansen
Heidi Hanson
Jean Hardenburg
Denise Harrison
Zenobia Hart
Andre Hayes
Brad Heiges
Theodore Henderson
June Hendrickson
Lillie Herring
Phyllis Hickerson
Carole Higginbotham
Janet Hill
Mildred Hill
Charles Hillis
Ann Hillman
Bette Hines
Margaret Hines
Hattie Hinant
Christine Hollis
Leonard Holsey
Nettie Hooks
Joan Horne
Jewell Horrell
Susan Horton
Florence Horwitz
Vivan Houk
Ray Huber
Diane Huff
Lillian Huff
Jacqueline Hughes
Lynell Hutcherson
Carolyn Israel
Aline Jackson
Eugene Jackson
Geraldine Jackson
Gloria Jackson
James Jackson
Lowell Jackson
Marie B. Jackson
Marie T. Jackson
Norma Jackson
Michael Jacobson
Ray Jacobson
Rolf Jacoby
Daryl James
Hilda James
Wade Jefferson
Evelyn Jeffries
Bruce Joggins
Alva Johnson
Antoinette Johnson
Claudette Johnson
Dorothy Johnson
Inga Johnson
Johnnie Johnson
Katie Johnson
Mary Johnson
Queenie Johnson
Ricky Johnson
Shirley Johnson
Thornton Johnson
DeElla Jones
Stella Jones
Jim Jonson
James Judd
Nancy Kaiser
Dan Kane
Eloise Kane

Lyn Karwaki
Thomas Karwaki
Gerry Katz
Veronica Keating
Thomas Keenan
Carol Kelley
Katherine Kelly
Michael Kelly
Irene Kemp
Vandy Kennedy
Carol King
Gladys King
Linda Kleckner
Carol Knutson
Barbara Kohrn
Nancy Kokus
Donald Krum
Judith Kusheloff
John Lackey
Susan Lamansdorf
Dolores Lamont
Ouida Larson
Margie Lawrence
Ruth Lawrence
Susan Lawrence
Christie Lazo
Eric Leeper
Frank Leone
Alicia Levinson
Elsa Levy
Davis Lewis
Judy Lewis
Larry Lewis
Stephen Lewis
Linda Lightfoot
Barbara Lisak
Mabel Littlepage
Al Lockhart
Etta H. McAfee
Mary H. McCormick
Annie McElrath
David McHenry
Jane McMahon
Annetta McMillan
Fredna Madison
Mary Madlin
Franklyn Malone
DeRadica Martin
John Martin
Phyllis Martin
Maud Massey
Pat Mathews
Martha Matland
Deborah Matovy
Willie Mayhand
Mae Melandry
Marilee Menard
Pauline Menes
Annie Mendoza
Allen Merkin
James Michael
Margaret Mickens
Emily Miller
Mercedes Miller
S. A. Moats
Lee Monroe
Martha Montgomery
Anita Moore
Doris Moore
Barbara Morgan
Marvin Moss
Edwina Murphy
Dan Murphy
Carol Murray
Lynn Murray
Eugene Myers
Raymond Myers
Adeeb Neam
Helen Neill
Geraldine Nessul

Mary Newman
Angelique Nickens
Francine Nisenoff
Alma Nixon
Tim Norris
Hal Northcott
Samson Ogunloye
Sandra O'Hara
Virginia Oldham
Pat Oliver
Crescentia O'Neal
Patricia O'Neal
Alvenia Owens
Cindy Palmer
Barbara Parrish
Phyllis Patillo
John Patton
Carol Paulette
Gertrude Payne
Gary Peade
LaVon Pendel
Andrea Phaneuf
Rosalie Phillips
Donna Phousouvanh
Flossie Pinkett
Angela Pisciotta
Frances Pisciotta
Ronald Piskorski
Judith Ponds
Arthur Pope
Riki Poster
Frank Pratka
Nicolee Prendergast
Catherine Procter
Dorothy Pryor
Barbara Quick
Cheryle Quick
Jess Quintero
Charles Reely
Frances Reynolds
Nadine Richards
Burnadette Richardson
Ann Richel
Virginia Ridearth
Kate Rinzler
Don Robinson
Fred Roberts
Jeannie Robinson
Ruth Robinson
Ted Rodgers
Danny Romano
Pearl Roper
Rosalind Rosenberg
Norma Rosenzweig
F. X. Rosica
Esther Rubinstein
Sally Ruskin
Shirley Salzman
Lucille Savage
Linda Scheffer
Mollie Schrick
Betty Schulman
Sue Schumacher
Lisa Sergio
Bill Shanley
Mary Shannon
Liz Sharlitt
Dolores Shea
Eva Shearin
Doug Shermen
Sigmund Shipp
Elizabeth Shoaf
Ginny Siegfried
Madeleine Sigel
Anna Simpson
Linda Smelley
Conrad Smith
Doris Jones Smith
Fan Smith

Flonnie Smith
Jean Smith
Marcia Smith
Mattie Smith
Paula Smith
Doris Solomon
Grant Sprandling
Barry Spodale
Breda Spriggs
Karen Stall
P. Steffey
Johelen Stern
June Stern
Eleanor Still
Ronnie Stone
Theresa Stone
Willie Stoney
Glenn Strahs
Margaret Strock
Shirley Sturghill
Graham Tancill
V. B. Tankersley
Catherine Taylor
Henrietta Taylor
Lillie Mae Taylor
John Ternus
Mary Terrell
Mary Thompson
Betsy Tibbs
Richard Trenk
Nadine Trowell
Evangeline Turner
John Turner
Peggy Tyler
Koko Unger
William Van Arsdel
John Van Brunt
Julie Van Brunt
Margaret Velarde
Gerry Vento
Nelson Vernelle
Tempe Vest
Michelle Vines
Wolf Von Eckhardt
Lisa Warner
Geraldine Washington
Evelyn Wartman
Ingrid Watson
Sam Watson
Vanessa Watson
Vivienne Watt
Annette Watts
Micki Weidenfeld
Lillian Weigel
Marc Weiss
Marjorie West
Robert White
Robert Lewis White
Helen Whytock
Teri Wiggams
Deborah Wilbanks
Ronnie Williams
Cathy Williammee
Alyce Williams
John Williams
Marvin Williams
Ronnie Williams
Steven Williams
Susan Williamson
Walter Wilson
William Wilson
Claudette Womack
Flora Wood
Pat Wood
Anne Woodbridge
Diane Wyatt
Jacqueline Yeager
Lillian Young
Susan Zeitz

ORGANIZATIONS

American Legion
Boy Scouts of America
Campfire Girls of America
College Democrats of
    American University
College Democrats of
    Georgetown University
College Democrats of
    George Washington University

College Democrats of
    Maryland University
Communication Workers of America
Department of Baptist Women
Elks Guard
Fairfax County Democratic Committee
George Mason University Students

Hamilton College Students
National Memorial Church
National Women's Democratic Club of
    Washington, D.C.
National Democratic Forum
Opportunity Industrialization Center
Stewardesses of America

Urban League Guild
Washington Center for
    Learning Alternatives
Washington Institute For Women
Women's Suburban Club in Bethesda
Young Men's Christian Association
Young Women's Christian Association

PATRONS, DONORS, AND CONTRIBUTORS

The 1977 Inaugural Committee wishes to thank the following patrons, donors, and contributors to the public and cultural events celebrating the inauguration of President Jimmy Carter and Vice President Walter F. Mondale:

PATRONS

Air Transport Association
 of America
American Family Life
 Assurance Company
American Trucking Association, Inc.
Armco Steel Corporation
Arthur Andersen and Company
Atlantic-Richfield Company
Avon Products, Inc.
The Bank of America
Bethlehem Steel Corporation
Cagles, Inc.
Cannon Mills Company
The Charles River Breeding
 Laboratories, Inc.
Chrysler Corporation
CIBA-Geigy Corporation

The Citizens and Southern
 National Bank of Atlanta
Coca-Cola, USA
Commerce Bank of Houston
Cox Enterprises, Inc.
Crawford and Company
Communication Workers of America
Delta Life Insurance Company
Delta Airlines
Eastern Airlines
Exxon Company, USA
Faith Investment Company, Inc.
Ford Motor Company
Franklin Mint Corporation
The Fulton National Bank
 of America
Fuqua Industries, Inc.
General Electric Company

General Motors Corporation
Genuine Parts, Inc.
The Grumman Corporation
Haskins and Sells
Industrial Systems Corporation
International Association
 of Machinists
 and Aerospace Workers
Ivan Allen Company
Kidder, Peabody and Company, Inc.
Knight-Ridder Newspapers
Marine Engineers Beneficial
 Association
The Marriott Corporation
Mobil Oil Corporation
National Association of Realtors
The National Bank of Georgia
Northeast Petroleum Industries, Inc.

Peat, Marwick, Mitchell
 and Company
Occidental Petroleum
RCA
The Riggs National Bank
Rockwell International
The Seagrams Company, Inc.
Silverstein and Mullens
Southern Pacific Company
The Tobacco Institute
United Auto Workers
Union Camp Corporation
U.S. League of Savings Associations
Winn-Dixie Stores, Inc.
Zehman Wolf Management, Inc.
Zehman Wolf Construction Company
American Security and Trust Bank

DONORS

AFL-CIO Building & Construction Trade
Agricultural & Dairy Education Political
 Trust
Alice Manufacturing Company
Allis-Chalmers
American Can Company
American Insurance Association
American Iron & Steel Institute
American Mining Congress
American Paper Institute
American Petroleum Institute
AMF Incorporated
Arnold Arnoff
Atlanta Life Insurance Company
AVCO Corporation
Avondale Mills
Bechtel Corporation
Bristol-Myers Company
Burlington Industries, Inc.
Robert Carson
Canteen Corporation
Anne Cox Chambers
James Cox Chambers
Robert Chambers
Clinton Mills
Collins & Aikman Corporation
Committee for Thorough Agricultural
 Political Education
Comprehensive Engineering Services
Computer Management Incorporated
Cone Mills Corporation
Coopers & Lybrand

Dixie Yarns, Inc.
Arthur J. Dover
Dundee Mills Incorporated
W. O. DuVal
Eastern Alloys, Inc.
The Eaton Corporation
EG&G, Inc.
Engineers Political Education Committee
Ernst & Ernst
Esmark Corporation
Fieldcrest Mills, Inc.
Fluor Corporation
Giant Food, Inc.
Goodyear Tire and Rubber Company
Government Services, Inc.
Harmony Grove Mills, Inc.
Greenwood Mills
Hughes Aircraft Company
I.U. International
Armand Hammer
Leon Hess
Hoffman-LaRoche, Inc.
Cynthia L. Howar
Inman Mills
INSILCO
International Union of Operating
 Engineers
ITT Corporation
Jackson Mills
Katherine Chambers Johnson
Johnson Wax Company
Kerr-McGee Corporation

King & Spalding
Killgallon Foundation
The LTV Corporation
Edward C. Levy
Lockheed-California Company
McDonnell Douglas Corporation
Robert McNeill
Macfield Texturing, Inc.
Philip Kramer
Mutual of Omaha
National Association of Broadcasters
National Machine Tool Builders
 Association
Nationwide Insurance Company
National Service Industries, Inc.
Opp Cotton Mills
Panhandle Eastern Pipeline Company
Panox Corporation
Powell, Goldstein, Frazer & Murphy
Price Waterhouse
Printing Industries of America, Inc.
Printpak, Inc.
Pullman, Inc.
Railway Progress Institute
Reeves Brothers, Inc.
Reynolds Metals Company
Robinson-Humphrey Co., Inc.
Sandoz Pharmaceuticals
William B. Schwartz, Jr.
G.D. Searle & Co.
Sears, Roebuck & Co.
Selig Enterprises, Inc.

Shaklee Corporation
Shaw Mudge
Shell Oil Company
Shuford Mills, Inc.
Southern Iron Co.
Southern Mills, Inc.
Southern Railway Company
Sperry & Hutchinson
Sperry Rand Corporation
Spring Mills, Inc.
Standard-Coosa-Thatcher Company
Standard Oil Company of Ohio
Standard Oil Company (Indiana)
Stanley Home Products, Inc.
Jim Stone
C. H. Stuart, Inc.
Margaretta Taylor
Texas Bank & Trust Company of Dallas
Texas Eastern Transmission Corporation
Touche Ross & Co.
Twentieth Century Fox Film Corporation
TRW, Inc.
Trans World Airlines, Inc.
Trust Company Bank
United Technologies Corporation
United Transportation Union
The Washington Post Company
Watkins Associated Industries, Inc.
Wellman Industries, Inc.
Western Union Corporation
Clyde A. Wheeler

CONTRIBUTORS

American Frozen Food Institute
Walter Anderson
Babcock & Wilcox Company
Rev. John P. Bartholomew
Frank Basko
Nellie H. Bass
Alan D. Becker
Bendix Corporation
Bershire Hathaway, Inc.
Serge Besoyan
D. A. Biglane
Blair Mills, Incorporated
Lewis F. Blenard, Jr.

Amy Bogdon
James R. Boring
Louise Bowser
Noah Bronkesh
Judy B. Brooks
John P. Buscher
Louise A. Chaculate
Philip Clifton
James M. Cloney
Ronald S. Cohen
Grover Collins
Vera E. Colyer
Combustion Engineering Inc.

Peter Conlon
Samuel L. Crane
R. B. Darling
John N. Davis
William DeGoode
Herbert Van Derlugt
Dover Textiles
Wilbert Entwistle
John Phillip Fayen
Fenn
Marie M. Ferrell
Fort Hill Investors Management Corp.
Fort Lincoln New Town Corporation

Fred F. French Investment Company, Inc.
Victor Frenkel
General Telephone & Electronics Service
 Corporation
Imogen Glover
H. Frederick Gonnerman
David H. Grambrell
Anita Girardi
Gertrude Grasser
Roman G. Gregory
Ivan F. Hall
Hardwood Plywood Manufacturing
 Association

CONTRIBUTORS (Continued)

Roger W. Helbig
Ardith A. Hilgerson
Randy King Hill
Irman Hiller
Hitt
Martha Hohman
Instrumentation Laboratory, Inc.
International Snowmobile Industry
    Association
Edna L. Irwin
Helen Johnson
Jodi J. Joyce
George Lielbriedis
Frances Lindenthal
Lorna Lockwood
Ray Majerus
Gladys Makela
Alice B. Martin
Herbert T. Margolis
Marc and Dorothy McGarvey
McGraw Hill, Inc.
J. Metz
Brian Miracle

John O. Mitchell
Jeanette Monahan
The Monocle Restaurant
Hays and Helen Moses
Stewart R. Mott
Peter E. Mulligan
Richard Myrick
National Electrical Manufacturers
    Association
National Soft Drink Association
Nesmith
Richard W. Neitz
Noble
Norton Company
Donald Novello
Loren Olson
Frances Perry
Mavis Petesch
John R. Pinkett, Inc.
Francis Plimpton
Fred W. Pope, Jr.
Allen Post
Potomac Electric & Power Company

Murray Pritchette
Agnes S. Riley
Jerome Rainey
Dr. G. R. Rankin
Gladys V. Ratke
O. B. Ratliff
Jack and Imogene Ramsey
Denis T. Rice
Agnes S. Riley
Jan Robbins
Jim Rowe
Safetran Systems Corporation
May Belle Scott
Rudolph O. Schmeichel
J. D. Shane
Smith, Bucklin & Associates, Inc.
David S. Smoak
A. L. Sorge
Kenneth C. Southard
Southern Airways
Spartan Mills
L. Jean Stengen
George A. Stoher

Harlan T. Strohl
Struthers Federated Democratic
    Womens Club
Mr. and Mrs. James Tedaldi
Thelma's Thimble
Lew Thomas
Callie Tilman
Alexander Thomson
Helen Thompson
Mr. and Mrs. T. G. Thompson
Gladys D. Tripp
United Telecommunications, Inc.
Andrew Valiska
Phyllis Vissman
Carole E. Wade
Mary A. Waddle
Washington Board of Realtors
Joseph Werner
John H. Whitley
Nell Whittle
Sharon J. Wright
Cheryle Yenovkian

PHOTO CREDITS   Photos credited to CMR are by Charles M. Rafshoon; those marked LC are from the Library of Congress, and those with the designation (AH) are courtesy of American Heritage Publishing Co. 8: Detail from Presidential flag, Herbert Loebel, courtesy of the White House (AH) 10: Portrait of George III, Colonial Williamsburg (AH) 11: Portrait of Washington, Pennsylvania Academy of the Fine Arts 12-13: View of Washington, D.C., Phelps Stokes Collection, New York Public Library (AH) 14: Jackson inaugural, LC (AH) 15: Jackson, George Eastman House (AH) 16: *Apotheosis of Lincoln*, LC (courtesy Newsweek Books) 17: *Apotheosis of Washington*, Henry Francis Du Pont Winterthur Museum (courtesy Newsweek Books) 18: Lincoln cartoon, LC (AH) 19: Theodore Roosevelt cartoon (AH) 20-21: Coolidge, LC (AH) 22: Franklin Roosevelt, Franklin Roosevelt Library (AH) 23: Chester Arthur, Cincinnati Historical Society (AH) 24: Truman and Eisenhower, UPI 25: Wilson and Colonel House, National Archives (AH) 27: Yalta Conference, Imperial War Museum, London (AH) 29: Kennedy, UPI 30: CMR 32-45: Photos from Carter family album, courtesy of CMR 46: Joe Dombroski 47: Top: CMR; Bottom: Stan Wayman, Life Magazine (Time, Inc.) 48-51: CMR 54-55: UPI 56-57: CMR 58: CMR 60-69: Photos from Mondale family album, courtesy of CMR 71: CMR 72: George Washington inaugural, Henry Francis Du Pont Winterthur Museum (courtesy Newsweek Books) 73: Washington in New York Harbor, National Gallery of Art, Gift of Edgar, William and Bernice Chrysler Garbisch 74: John Adams, Metropolitan Museum of Art, Gift of William H. Huntington (AH) 75: Harrison inaugural, Anne S.K. Brown Military Collection (AH) 76: Buchanan inaugural, LC (AH) 77: Lincoln inaugural, LC (AH) 78: Rutherford and Lucy Hayes, Hayes Memorial Library (AH) 79: Garfield inaugural, LC (AH) 80-81: Hoover and Roosevelt, from left: Wide World, UPI, Franklin Roosevelt Library (AH) 114: Robert E. Lee monument, David White, Black Star

AUTHORS FOR THIS BOOK   **Alex Haley** is the author of the current best-seller, *Roots*, which reconstructs the history of the Haley family since the arrival of its early ancestors here—in chains, aboard a slaver.   **James David Barber**, Chairman of the Political Science Department at Duke University, is the author, among other works, of *Presidential Character*.   **James Dickey**, one of the best known contemporary Southern poets, is also a novelist.   **H. Brandt Ayers** is the editor of the Anniston Star, Anniston, Alabama and the author (with others) of *You Can't Eat Magnolias*, about the resurgence of the South.   **Richard M. Ketchum**, biographer of George Washington and Will Rogers, is editor of *Country Journal* and a former editorial director of American Heritage Publishing Company.   **Hal Gulliver**, who is working on a book about the Carter Presidential campaign, is editor of the *Atlanta Constitution*.   **William Barry Furlong**, a Washington-based journalist, is the author most recently of a book about headache, *More Than Two Aspirin*.

ACKNOWLEDGEMENTS   The editors would like to thank the following for their help in preparing this book: Peggy Buckwalter, American Heritage Publishing Co.; The Aviation Section, United States Park Police; Bill Cochrane and Ray Nelson, Joint Congressional Inaugural Committee; Marya Dalrymple; Abe Dulberg, Reiter-Dulberg Labs; Oscar Dystel, Marc Jaffe and Jean Highland of Bantam Books; Al Garfin, Newsweek Books; Lilyan Glusker; Mary and Juergen Haber; Kendra Ho; Michael Klos; Carl Lau; George Love; Brian McGean; Jack Newman; Nikon Professional Services; Dev O'Neill; Cal Sacks; Lisa Suarez; Kate and Elizabeth Tomkievicz and their daddy, Alex; Eloise Vega; Donna Whiteman; Paula Ehrlich, Dale Hulshizer; and for editorial counsel: Prof. James McGregor Burns, Roy Reed, Lester Bernstein, Steve Blickstein and Herbert Gandel.

Color separations and cover printing by Collier Graphics, New York; Composition by Compo-Set Typographers, Inc., New York; Paper supplied by Lindenmeyr Paper Corporation, New York; Printed by Meehan-Tooker, East Rutherford, New Jersey; Bound by A. Horowitz & Sons, Fairfield, New Jersey

Staff for this book

THE 1977 INAUGURAL COMMITTEE

PROJECT DIRECTOR   *Gerald M. Rafshoon*
ASSISTANT PROJECT DIRECTOR   *McAdory Lipscomb*
TECHNICAL PRODUCER   *Kevin Gorman*
DIRECTOR OF PHOTOGRAPHY   *Charles M. Rafshoon*

DUOBOOKS, INC.

EDITORIAL AND DESIGN DIRECTOR   *Irwin Glusker*
PRODUCTION DIRECTOR   *Henry Horowitz*
EDITOR   *Shirley Tomkievicz*
PICTURE EDITOR   *Laurie Platt Winfrey*
ASSISTANT EDITOR   *Jacqueline Mason*
LAYOUT DESIGN   *Christian von Rosenvinge*
LAYOUT   *Kristen Reilly*
                                 Constance T. Timm
                                 Walter Romanski